The Six Day War and the Yom Kippur War: The History of the Military Conflicts that Established Israel as a Superpower in the Middle East
By Charles River Editors

A picture of Egyptian President Gamal Abdel Nasser shortly before the Six Day War

About Charles River Editors

Charles River Editors is a boutique digital publishing company, specializing in bringing history back to life with educational and engaging books on a wide range of topics. Keep up to date with our new and free offerings with this 5 second sign up on our weekly mailing list, and visit Our Kindle Author Page to see other recently published Kindle titles.

We make these books for you and always want to know our readers' opinions, so we encourage you to leave reviews and look forward to publishing new and exciting titles each week.

Introduction
The Six Day War and Yom Kippur War

Picture of Israeli soldiers next to a destroyed Egyptian aircraft during the Six Day War

"We shall not attack any State so long as it does not wage war against us. But anyone attacking us will meet with our full power of self-defense and our capacity to defeat his forces." – Israeli Prime Minister Levi Eshkol

In May 2011, President Barack Obama gave speeches about the Middle East that discussed the Israeli-Palestinian conflict, using terms like "final status issues," "1967 lines with mutually agreed swaps," and "demographic realities." Obama's speeches were strongly denounced by both the Palestinians and the Israelis, while political commentators across the world debated what Obama's speeches actually meant.

Welcome to the Middle East conflict, a conflict that is technically 63 years old and counting but has its roots in over 2,000 years of history. With so much time and history, the peace process has become laden with unique, politically sensitive concepts like the right of return, contiguous borders, secure borders, demilitarized zones, and security requirements, with players like the Quartet, Palestinian Authority, Fatah, Hamas, the Arab League and Israel. Over time, it has become exceedingly difficult for even sophisticated political pundits and followers to keep track of it all.

Despite losing the 1948 war, Arab nations throughout the Middle East had still refused to recognize Israel's right to exist. After the Suez Crisis, Egyptian leader Gamal Abdel Nasser envisioned creating a unified Arab world, commonly referred to as pan-Arabism. Nasser was the consummate pan-Arab leader in the 1960s, positioning himself as the leader of the Arab world through increasing incitement against Israel with rhetoric.

Israel found itself in possession of more land after 1948 than envisioned by the U.N. Partition

Plan, but the Green Line still left it less than 10 miles wide in some positions. In the summer of 1967, the armies of Jordan and Syria mobilized near Israel's borders, while Egypt's army mobilized in the Sinai Peninsula just west of the Gaza Strip. Combined, the Arab armies numbered over 200,000 soldiers.

In early June 1967, the Israelis captured Jordanian intelligence that indicated an invasion was imminent, and at 08h10 on June 5, 1967, the Israel Broadcasting Authority aired an Israeli Defense Force communique. "Since the early hours of this morning," it read, "heavy fighting has been taking place on the southern front between Egyptian armored and aerial forces, which moved against Israel, and our forces, which went into action to check them." This was followed up a little over two hours later by a publicly aired message to the armed forces of Israel, released by Israeli Minister of Defense Moshi Dayan in his first day in office. "We have no aims of conquest," was Dayan' simple message. "Our only aim is to frustrate the attempt of the Arab armies to conquer our country, and to sever and crush the ring of blockade and aggression which has been created around us."

By then, the Israeli Air Force had been in action over the skies of Egypt since 07h45 that morning, and as a consequence, almost the entire Egyptian Air Force lay smoldering on the tarmacs of various forward Egyptian airbases. Having neutralized Egypt's air strike potential in a matter of hours, the IAF then began to turn its attention to Jordan, Iraq and Syria, as IDF ground forces, back in the Sinai, moved in to take care of the more punishing business of destroying Egyptian ground forces.

These public protestations, declaring that Israel desired only peace and would initiate no aggressive action against any neighbor, rang more than a little hollow in the face of all of this, but in the context of Israeli national survival, it had been agreed that offense was defense. The only rational defensive doctrine, bearing in mind Israel's extreme vulnerability, was to take the war to the Arabs. Only in this way could the comparatively diminutive Israeli armed forces have any hope of victory.

Over the next six days, the Israelis overwhelmed the Egyptians in the west, destroying thousands of tanks and capturing the Gaza Strip and the entire Sinai Peninsula. At the same time, Israel drove the Jordanians out of Jerusalem and the West Bank, and it captured the Golan Heights from Syria near the border of Lebanon. In the span of a week, Israel had tripled the size of the lands it controlled. Israel had gone from less than 10 miles wide in some spots to over 200 miles wide from the Sinai Peninsula to the West Bank. Israel also unified Jerusalem.

The results of the Six Day War created several issues that have still not been resolved in the Middle East. Israel now found itself in possession of territories that were the home of over a million Arabs. Of these territories, Israel officially annexed only East Jerusalem and the Golan Heights, leaving the inhabitants of the West Bank, Sinai Peninsula, and Gaza Strip in limbo regarding citizenship status.

Despite attempts to create peace, the Arab nations refused to recognize Israel, and Israel refused to withdraw from any of the land it captured in 1967. After conquering the territories, Israel began encouraging Jewish settlement in the new territories. In the 1970s, more than 10,000 Jews moved into the West Bank, Gaza Strip, Golan Heights, East Jerusalem, and the Sinai Peninsula, a figure that grew to over 100,000 by the early '80s and is now over 500,000 today. Some in Israel note that Jewish settlements in 1967 had simply reestablished Jewish communities in places they had lived prior to 1948, including Jerusalem, Hebron, and Gush Etzion, as well as Gaza City in the Gaza Strip. They also argue that the legal status of the territories was never officially determined due to the Palestinian rejection of the U.N. Partition

Plan. Still others assert that Israel's settlements do not breach international law or the Geneva Convention because it fought the Six Day War in self-defense and did not forcibly transfer civilian populations onto occupied territories. However, despite those arguments, the vast majority of the world considers Jewish settlements on land captured by Israel in 1967 to be illegal, including the United Nations, the International Court of Justice, and the international community.

On October 6, 1973, Syria and Egypt caught Israel off guard during the Jewish holy holiday of Yom Kippur, surprise attacking the Sinai Peninsula and Golan Heights. Although they initially made gains, the Israelis turned the tide within a week, going on the counteroffensive and winning the war within 3 weeks.

The Yom Kippur War was the last concerted invasion of Israel by conventional Arab armies, but it underscored how entangled the West and the Soviet Union had gotten in the region. The British and French had been allied with Israel in the 1950s, including during the Suez Canal War, and the United States assisted Israel by providing weapons as early as the 1960s. As a way of counteracting Western influence, the Soviets developed ties with the Arab nations.

After the Yom Kippur War, President Jimmy Carter's administration sought to establish a peace process that would settle the conflict in the Middle East, while also reducing Soviet influence in the region. On September 17, 1978, after secret negotiations at the presidential retreat Camp David, Egyptian President Anwar Sadat and Israeli Prime Minister Menachem Begin signed a peace treaty between the two nations, in which Israel ceded the Sinai Peninsula to Egypt in exchange for a normalization of relations, making Egypt the first Arab adversary to officially recognize Israel. Carter also tried to create a peace process that would settle the rest of the conflict vis-à-vis the Israelis and Palestinians, but it never got off the ground.

For the Camp David Accords, Begin and Sadat won the Nobel Peace Prize. Begin had once been a leader of the paramilitary group Irgun, while Sadat had succeeded Nasser. Ultimately, the peace treaty may have cost Sadat his life: he was assassinated in 1981 by fundamentalist military officers during a victory parade.

The Six Day War and the Yom Kippur War: The History of the Military Conflicts that Established Israel as a Superpower in the Middle East looks at two of the most decisive events of the 20th century for the region. Along with and a bibliography, you will learn about the Six Day War and Yom Kippur War like never before.

The Six Day War and the Yom Kippur War: The History of the Military Conflicts that Established Israel as a Superpower in the Middle East

About Charles River Editors

Introduction

   The Path to War

   Egypt

   Jordan

   Syria

   The Aftermath

   Superpower Involvement in the Six Day War

   The Occupied Territories

   Preamble to the Yom Kippur War

   The Israeli Illusion

   A New Strategy

   The Enemy

   The Start of the Yom Kippur War

   A Reversal of Fortunes

   The Aftermath

   Online Resources

   Further Reading

Free Books by Charles River Editors

Discounted Books by Charles River Editors

The Path to War
"We shall not enter Palestine with its soil covered in sand; we shall enter it with its soil saturated in blood." – President Gamal Nasser

Restrictions imposed on Jewish immigration to Palestine remained in place throughout World War II and continued in the aftermath, even as millions of displaced Jews throughout Europe sought sanctuary from the horror of the Holocaust, the true extent of which was only then being fully appreciated. There was an obvious unwillingness on the part of many East European Jews to return to their ruined communities, and a mass movement of Jews within and out of Europe began. The British established a quota of 18,000 a year, which all but made legal immigration impossible for the hundreds of thousands of Jews trying to get into Palestine. Thousands were intercepted and interred in camps in Cyprus.

A Jewish underground movement began to facilitate illegal immigration from Europe and elsewhere to Palestine, under the codename Aliyah Bet. The program, in fact, began before the war, as the British began attempting to limit Jewish arrivals in order to try and defuse tensions, but it was curtailed during the war since maritime transit was impossible under wartime conditions. The effort to accelerate Jewish immigration was naturally motivated by the horrors of the Holocaust and European anti-Semitism in general, but it was also part of a strategy to improve the demographic balance as much as possible in favor of the Zionists at a time when Zionist militias were beginning to exchange blows with the British Army. The British did what they could to enforce the restrictions imposed in the 1939 White Paper, but a great many immigrant ships sidestepped the blockade, and tens of thousands of Jews were able to enter Palestine illegally and settle.

Hostilities between Arabs and Jews, and between Zionist Militias and the British Army, began again in earnest after the war, and they escalated quickly. The British soon found themselves under pressure from all sides, and the United States, under President Harry S. Truman, urged the lifting of Jewish immigration restrictions and limits on Jewish land purchases. This led to the establishment of an Anglo-American Committee of Inquiry, which, in April 1946, opened the way for the legal entry of 100,000 Jewish Holocaust survivors and the rescinding of restrictions of land sales to Jews. It further suggested that the territory of Palestine be neither Jewish nor Arab, urging instead a continuation of international trusteeship.

These recommendations, forlorn in their optimism, triggered violent demonstrations in the neighboring Arab states, and some called for a Jihad and an annihilation of all European Jews in Palestine. At the end of 1946, upwards of 600,000 Jews were known to reside in the Mandate of Palestine, compared to a population of 1,300,000 Arabs.

Britain, now facing the reality of decolonization and the winding down of the British Empire, rapidly lost its appetite to deal with what was an increasing intractable problem, so in February 1947, the British announced their intention to relinquish the governing mandate over the territory of Palestine. By then, the League of Nations had been superseded by the United Nations as the global governing body, and the matter was therefore submitted to the General Assembly to be resolved. The British anticipated a single-state solution and was quietly hopeful that the Arab majority population would carry the day. The United States, on the other hand, now more forceful in international affairs, pressed for a solution more favorable to the Jews.

In May 1947, a United Nations Special Committee, UNSCOP, was established to investigate and make recommendations for the future of Palestine. The Jewish Agency lobbied for Jewish representation on the committee, and also, in a sign of a more hawkish and confident Zionist mood, for the exclusion of both Britain and Arab countries. It also pressed hard for the committee to include visits to camps where Holocaust survivors were interned in Europe as part of its brief. The Arab states, on the other hand, convinced that Arab statehood in Palestine was under threat, and unwilling to acknowledge the United Nations justification over the matter, argued that the rule of Palestine should revert to its inhabitants, in accordance with the provisions of the Charter of the United Nations, or that the matter should be put before an International Court. The Arab Higher Committee, therefore, refused to cooperate with UNSCOP.

In August 1947, a majority report of the United Nations Special Committee recommended that the region be partitioned into separate Arab and Jewish states. This was followed, on November 29, 1947, by a vote of the United Nations General Assembly that ratified the plan, and put it into existence. The terms of the plan were contained in Resolution 181, and the most important result was that the land would be partitioned in such a way as to ensure that each state would have a majority of its own population. Nonetheless, inevitably, some Jewish settlements would fall within the proposed Arab state, while hundreds of thousands of Palestinian Arabs would become part of the proposed Jewish state. The area designated for the Jewish state would also be slightly larger than the Arab state, in the expectation of accelerated Jewish immigration at the moment that Jewish autonomy was achieved. Jerusalem and Bethlehem would become international zones under United Nations administration.

Each state would comprise three major sections, linked by extraterritorial crossroads, and the Arabs would also gain an enclave at Jaffa. With about 32% of the population, the Jews would be allocated 56% of the land, containing a population of roughly 499,000 Jews and 438,000 Arabs, but most of this territory comprised the Negev Desert of the south. The Arabs would get 42% of the land, with a population of 818,000 Palestinian Arabs and some 10,000 Jews.

While that partition sounds lopsided at first glance, it's important to recall, as Zionists at the time pointed out, that Transjordan, which was granted independence by the British in 1946, had comprised 75% of the entire land under British control, meaning the proposed Jewish state would end up comprising less than 15% of the entire Mandate while two Arab countries got the other 85%.

Publicly, the Zionist Jewish leadership accepted this plan, acknowledging it as "the indispensable minimum." The Arabs, on the other hand, rejected the plan entirely, regarding the whole process, including the General Assembly vote, as an international betrayal.

Ongoing tensions and clashes flared into organized communal violence at the moment that the General Assembly vote was made public and the partition plan was formally adopted. Bombings, killings and riots became a matter of daily life on both sides, although on the whole, the Jews tended to more frequently be on the receiving end. According to Israel Galili, Chief of Staff of the Haganah, "As far as we know, it is the Mufti's belief that there is no better way to 'start things off' than by means of terror, isolated bombs thrown into crowds leaving movie theaters on Saturday nights. That will start the ball rolling. For no doubt the Jews will react, and as a reaction to a reaction there will be an outbreak in another place ... until the whole country will be stirred up, trouble will be incited, and the neighboring Arab countries will be compelled to start a 'holy war' to assist the Palestinian Arabs."

Clearly, the Higher Arab Council hoped, through an organized campaign of violence, that a wider regional conflict would be sparked. Attacks, however, were often random and uncoordinated, utilizing poorly armed, ill-trained and disorganized militias, contrasting sharply to the Haganah, which, although numerically inferior, was motivated, organized, trained, and reasonably well-armed. In fact, the importation of armaments, especially heavy arms, was difficult, if not impossible, so long as the British were in substantive control of Palestine. In

December 1947, Zionist leader David Ben-Gurion ordered the Haganah to begin transitioning into a regular army in expectation of an escalation of the violence, but the emphasis tended to be on the training and organization of manpower, and the establishment of communications networks and command and control. Meanwhile, arms were purchased overseas and held in readiness to be introduced as soon as the British had relinquished control. Soon afterwards, Zionist forces abandoned their defensive posture and began staging retaliatory raids and offensive actions against hostile Palestinian villages and mounting regular assassinations of Palestinian militia and civic leaders.

David Ben-Gurion giving the declaration of Israel's independence

On May 14, 1948, Ben-Gurion, as the head of the Jewish Agency, declared the establishment of the State of Israel, and the following day the British Mandate of Palestine officially expired. As the British packed up and left the territory, no doubt breathing a sigh of relief, the armies of four Arab nations – Egypt, Syria, Transjordan and Iraq – entered what had been British Mandatory Palestine, triggering the 1948 Arab-Israeli War. Ostensibly, the Arab forces embarked on the war to reverse the creation of Israel in defense of the Palestinians, but it is also likely that each held its own territorial ambitions, and it is probably unlikely that an Arab victory would have resulted in the formation of a Palestinian state.

Given the numbers on each side, it seemed the new Israeli state was facing staggering odds, so it's no surprise that what followed was quite sobering to Israel's Arab neighbors. In less than a year, they would be repelled and defeated with comparative ease, which, bearing in mind the disparity of weapons and manpower that the two sides wielded, shocked them to the core.

During May and June of 1948, when the fighting was at its most intense, the balance was very much in doubt, but as arms shipments began to reach Israeli fighting formations, the Israeli Defense Force gradually began to dominate the battlefield. Much of the reason for this was a lack of tactical coordination between the individual Arab armies, each of which fought an individual campaign in individual sectors.

The Israelis began pressing their advantages on both land and air by the fall of 1948, bombing foreign capitals like Damascus while overrunning Arab armies locally. In towns like Ramat Rachel and Deir Yassin, close quarter combat in villages led to civilian casualties and charges of massacres. In particular, the Jewish assault on Deir Yassin, which led to the death of about 50 Palestinians, is often labeled a massacre by the Palestinians, while the Israelis asserted that house-to-house combat made fighting difficult. Regardless, Palestinians who heard of the news of Jewish attacks on places like Deir Yassin were afraid for their lives and began to flee their homes. At the same time, Palestinians were encouraged by commanders of the Arab armies to clear out of the area until after they could defeat Israel. Palestinians and Jews had been fighting since 1947, and over 250,000 Palestinians had already fled their homes by the time the war had started. It is unclear how many Palestinians fled from Jewish forces and how many left voluntarily, but by the end of the war, over 700,000 Palestinians had fled from their homes. Meanwhile, nearly 800,000 Jews had been forcibly expelled from their homes in nations throughout the Middle East, leading to an influx of Jews at the same time Palestinians were leaving.

By late 1948, Israel was on the offensive. That December, the U.N. General Assembly passed Resolution 194, which declared that under a peace agreement, "refugees wishing to return to their homes and live in peace with their neighbors should be permitted to do so," and "compensation should be paid for the property of those choosing not to return."

Protracted peace talks began late in January 1949, resulting in individual armistices signed with each defeated power. Iraq did not sign an armistice, instead merely opting to withdraw its forces. The territory once known as Palestine was divided into three parts, each under a different political regime. Israel now encompassed over 77% of the lands that were part of the U.N. Partition Plan, while Jordan held East Jerusalem and the West Bank, and Egypt occupied the coastal strip adjacent to the city of Gaza.

Across Israel's borders, Arab nationalism surged, especially in the form of Gamal Abdel Nasser, the Egyptian president now most associated with pan-Arab nationalism. Nasser rose to power in the aftermath of a military coup that deposed the pro-British rule of King Farouk, who the Egyptian military blamed for Egypt's poor performance in 1948. Nasser antagonized the West, and in particular Britain and France, with ongoing threats to nationalize the Suez Canal. Egyptian forces remained in occupation of Gaza City and the area around it, and sporadic attacks, initiated by both sides, had been ongoing since 1948. Nasser made no secret of his antipathy towards Israel and his ambition to destroy it, and at the same time he was anxious to be released from a 1936 Anglo-Egyptian Treaty that granted the British the right to station troops in the Suez Canal Zone. He was also enraged at the refusal of the United States to release funds for the construction of the Aswan Dam. Furthermore, he blockaded the Gulf of Aqaba and the Straits of Tiran, cutting off Israeli access to the Red Sea, which was by any standards a declaration of war.

Nasser

On July 26, 1956, Nasser made good his threat and nationalized the Suez Canal, setting in motion the events of the Suez Crisis of that year. The British adopted a hawkish approach, deciding on a military response, and for this they sought the support of the French, who believed that Nasser was supporting rebels in the French colony of Algeria. Israel, anxious for the sake of its own border security to push back the Egyptians, also came on board. The Israelis moved first, occupying Gaza before moving into the Sinai Peninsula and finally seizing control of Sharm el-Sheikh and reopening the Gulf of Aqaba. Two days after the Israelis, Anglo-French forces went into action and achieved their objective of securing the Canal Zone.

The Soviets, coming to Nasser's defense, issued nuclear threats, which prompted the President Dwight Eisenhower's administration not only to warn the Soviets against involvement, but also to issue stern warnings the French, British, and Israelis to cease and desist. British and French forces were obliged to withdraw from the region, which they did by December 1956, and by March 1957, Israel had withdrawn all forces from the Sinai.

The Israelis hoped for more as a consequence of the 1956 war, but in the end, a costly series of operations had resulted in very little strategic gain. They remained alert to the possibility, however, and established a broad strategic plan that envisaged the seizure of territory to the north and south as a security buffer. The Israeli Defense Force absorbed the lessons of 1956 and embarked on a program of rearmament and professionalization. Israel's main arms supplier at this time was France, from which the IDF sourced small arms, tanks and assault aircraft, including the all-important Dassault Mirage III.

Oren Rozen's picture of a Dassault Mirage III

On all sides, however, and in particular Egypt, the Arab states were doing the same, capitalizing on their alliances with the Soviet Union to comprehensively rearm and reequip. All the while, raids and reprisals between Palestinian guerrilla groups (Fedayeen) and the IDF continued.

All sides in the Middle East were building towards a definitive war. Nasser was probably the greatest driver of renewed warfare in the Middle East. His ultra-nationalist position, virulent anti-Israeli platform, and pan-Arab ambitions, as well as an exaggerated faith in the power of his Soviet-supplied armed forces, gave him arguably the greatest interest in war. He ordered a full mobilization in May 1967, stationing some 100,000 troops in the Sinai Peninsula and expelling the United Nations monitoring force. In addition, he once again closed the Straits of Tiran in another unmistakable precursor to war.

At this point, Israel was just under two decades old, and its Arab opponents, primarily Syria and Egypt, remained deeply shocked. It was not only the utter humiliation of a vast Arab military alliance at the hands of an ad hoc and barely constituted Israeli army in 1948, but the fact that Israel then blossomed into being when the expectation had been that the very idea would be stamped out by Arab might before it was even born. Thereafter, Israel continued to grow and flourish in a geopolitical zone held to be Arab. It was an insult to Arab nationalism, and a daily reminder of one of the most spectacular military reverses suffered in the region to date.

The annihilation of Israel, the utter removal of the Jewish state from the map of the Middle East, and the expunging of its memory because the single, unifying Arab foreign policy objective, and one of the very few policies that every participating state complied with. Arab verbiage on the subject began in a tone of implacable hostility, and it had continued as the region entered the era of the Cold War, which brought the complex patronage of East and West into an increasingly insecure area.

In the 1960s, the primary Israeli defense concern lay in the lack of strategic depth left over from the armistice lines of the 1948 war. East Jerusalem and the West Bank were Jordanian territory, and the potential for hostile action against Israel grew as Palestinian guerrillas (Fedayeen) began to stage incursions into Israel under the protection of the Jordanian authorities and Egyptian and Iraqi troops stationed in Jordan. These attacks mainly targeted soft Jewish civilian targets, and moderate or non-aligned Arabs.

In 1964, the Arab League met in Cairo and formed the **Palestine Liberation Organization** (PLO), which intended to "liberate" Palestine and drive the Jews into the sea. At the time, Egypt and Jordan occupied the Gaza Strip and West Bank respectively, which the PLO had no interest in contesting. The PLO Charter stated, "This Organization does not exercise any territorial sovereignty over the West Bank in the Hashemite Kingdom of Jordan, or on the Gaza Strip." Although the PLO became the most famous Palestinian organization, it actually consisted of several independently operating groups. The most noteworthy of them was **Fatah**, which had been founded in 1956 and had been conducting attacks on Israeli targets since its inception. Among the members of Fatah was **Yasser Arafat**, who would soon become the most visible face of the PLO. Other main groups within the PLO included Popular Front for the Liberation of Palestine and the Popular Democratic Front for the Liberation of Palestine, which essentially were militant groups.

The same problems existed in the north along Israel's common border with Syria – Syria then commanded the Golan Heights, overlooking the agricultural heartland of Israel – and in the south, where Egypt controlled Gaza and the Sinai Peninsula. The 1956 war with Egypt had presented the opportunity to gain some depth in the Sinai, but subsequent diplomatic pressures had forced a withdrawal, and thereafter, the Israeli defense establishment remained concerned and alert to the direct, three-dimensional military threat posed by all of Israel's neighbors.

The level of threat grew steadily through the early 1960s as Nasser cemented his pro-Soviet position and began acquiring injections of Soviet financial support and weapons, with which the Egyptian army and air force were modernized and expanded. From 1956-1967, an estimated $2 billion USD in Soviet military aid found its way to the Middle East, including some 1,700 tanks, 2,400 artillery pieces, 500 jet fighters and thousands of Soviet military advisers, about 43 percent of which was directed to Egypt.[1]

Israel, on the other hand, relied almost entirely on France as an arms supplier, but with the election in 1958 of General Charles de Gaulle as President of France, a cooling of diplomatic relations began. De Gaulle was no particular friend of Israel, and he guided France towards a more Arab-friendly position, in recognition of increasing Arab control of global petroleum reserves. The sale of French weapons and war materiel to the Middle East was banned, at a time when Israel was the only recipient of French arms in the Middle East. The British were more sympathetic to Israel, but they too were forced to consider their diplomatic relationship with the Arab oil producing countries, so they limited their diplomatic engagement with Israel.

In 1966, with Soviet encouragement, Nasser brokered on behalf of Egypt a mutual defense pact with Syria, committing either territory to the defense of the other in the case of Israeli aggression.

All of this contributed to a growing sense of vulnerability in Israel, but there were other peripheral issues that also helped raise diplomatic tensions in the region. One such was the Arab

---

[1] Figures provided by the *Britain Israel Communications and Research Center.*

League's plans to divert the water of the Jordan River away from Israel, and no secret was made of the fact that this would be undertaken as part of a wider destabilization effort. On April 7, 1967, a clash took place between Syrian and Israeli forces that began with an artillery duel and ended in an air battle in which six Syrian MiG-21s were shot down.

In May 1967, an erroneous and perhaps deliberately destabilizing Soviet intelligence report was made available to Egyptian intelligence, indicating a large-scale Israeli troop build-up massing on Israel's northern border in preparation to attack Syria. The Israelis denied this and offered diplomatic guarantees, but Nasser began his own force build-up in the Sinai. Four Egyptian brigades were deployed on the peninsula, and Nasser ordered the 3,400 strong United Nations peacekeeping force to vacate their positions on Israel's southern border. The UN Emergency Force, or UNEF, had been established in the region after the 1956 Sinai/Suez conflict, and United Nations Secretary-General, U Thant, complied with this directive with very little, if any protest. He bypassed the General Assembly, which was contrary to protocol at the very least.

This established a very dangerous precedent on the peninsula, and on the part of Egypt, it certainly was difficult to see it as anything less than an unambiguous provocation. Egyptian forces were now in a position to mobilize against Israel without hindrance in the Sinai, and by having ordered the United Nations around, Nasser's prestige within the Arab League was considerably enhanced.

Meanwhile, Israel had established a number of clear criteria under which it would consider itself at war, or under the threat of war from its neighbors. These included the blockading of the Straits of Tiran, which would effectively shut the Israeli Port of Eilat, on the Gulf of Aqaba, off from international shipping; the deployment of Iraqi troops into Jordan; the signing of an Egyptian/Jordanian defense agreement; and the withdrawal of the UN emergency force. The latter's withdrawal, and the alacrity with which it was undertaken, was certainly seen by Israel as a large measure of Egypt's seriousness, but on May 22, 1967, Nasser went further by blockading the Straits of Tiran to Israeli shipping. At the very least, this was a violation of international law, and the Israeli defense establishment began to take the threat of war very seriously indeed.

United States President Lyndon B. Johnson, later commenting on events as they unfolded during that tense spring of 1967, observed, "If a single act of folly was more responsible for this explosion than any other, it was the arbitrary and dangerous announced decision that the Straits of Tiran would be closed." Nonetheless, the White House urged restraint, offering the assistance of an international flotilla, Operation *Red Sea Regatta*, to challenge it, but in the end, largely thanks to American and Soviet naval sparring in the Mediterranean, this initiative never got off the ground.

President Johnson

Despite having raised tensions with flawed and largely unverified intelligence reports, the Soviet position was initially ambiguous, and no overt encouragement was expressed towards Egypt over the closure of the Straits of Tiran. A *Pravda* article that appeared three days after the closure was limited to observing that Israel had not enjoyed a right of access to the Gulf of Aqaba prior to 1956, and so, therefore, she had no supportable claim to access now. This was followed on May 23 by an official Soviet dispatch that repeated accusations that Israel was preparing for an attack against Syria, warning that the result of such an action would not only be a united and dramatic Arab response but also that "strong opposition" might be expected from the Soviet Union and all other peace-loving states. In fact, Soviet support for the Arabs remained equivocal throughout, and the only clear commitment was an undertaking to offer direct Soviet support to the Arabs only if direct U.S. support was offered to Israel.

In the wake of Nasser's actions, Israeli Prime Minister Levi Eshkol issued an official statement warning that Egyptian interference with Israeli shipping would be regarded as an act of aggression. Despite this, Eshkol resisted the hawks in both his government and defense establishment for several weeks, holding out against a preemptive strike without expressed American support, and certainly against the risk of being internationally judged as being the aggressor.

Eshkol

Nasser, however, maintained a steady outflow of aggressive rhetoric. In a speech delivered on May 26, he stated, "Recently we have felt strong enough that if we enter a battle with Israel, with God's help, we could triumph. On this basis we decided to take actual steps…taking over Sharm ash-Shaykh…meant that we were ready to enter a general war with Israel…and our objective would be to destroy Israel."

A few days later, further military defense pacts were signed between Egypt, Jordan and Iraq, theoretically unifying the forces of all three against Israel, and adding to a definitive breach of the conditions for war that Israel had already spelled out. King Hussein of Jordan, generally the least belligerent of the Arab "frontline" members, marked the moment with the following observation: "All of the Arab armies now surround Israel. The UAR, Iraq, Syria, Jordan, Yemen, Lebanon, Algeria, Sudan, and Kuwait…there is no difference between one Arab people and another, no difference between one Arab army and another."

Nasser and King Hussein of Jordan

This sort of talk, at least in the context of local military realities, was probably not to be taken very seriously since Arab unity had remained throughout Israel's short existence more of a talking point than a strategic reality. The fact nonetheless remained, however, that Israel, with a small army mostly comprised of citizen reserves, was facing the combined threat of several Arab nations, each committed to the single objective of its destruction. At that point, the Israeli Defense Force, while confident that victory was possible, was not yet quite so convinced of its tactical superiority as to believe that defeat was impossible.

The ongoing mobilization of Egyptian forces in the Sinai was the source of continuing anxiety in Tel Aviv, and the sort of threatening media and public language emanating from Egypt, from the Syrian defense establishment, and from the ranks of the PLO, all seemed to confirm a united and imminent Arab threat.

Israeli Prime Minister Levi Eshkol eventually succumbed to political and public pressure. Seeing the writing on the wall, on June 5, 1967, he relinquished the portfolio of Minister of Defense, which he held, to Moshe Dayan, signalling that war had become inevitable.

Dayan

Egypt

"Israel will not be alone unless it decides to go alone." - President Lyndon B. Johnson

In 1967, the Israeli Air Force consisted of about 260 combat aircraft (mostly French/Dassault Aviation), although figures in this regard vary depending on the source. Combined Arab air forces consisted of some 341 Egyptian, 90 Syrian, and 18 Jordanian combat aircraft, most of which were Soviet-supplied (although the Jordanians did operate a flight of British Hawker Hunters). Bearing this in mind, Israeli defence planners considered the Egyptian long-range bomber fleet, and the prior deployment of Egyptian forces in the Sinai, as the clearest and most imminent threat.

Israeli intelligence, a growing force among international intelligence agencies, had established that the Arabs in general, and Egypt in particular, were poorly prepared for war. There were many reasons for this, but in the case of Egypt, the politicization of the army and the politicization of war undermined both. Nasser, for example, was suspicious of the educated elite of his nation, and he avoided the involvement in the military of any element potentially hostile to him, fearing a potential coup. This tended to result in a lower quality of junior and mid-level command, and a lower technical appreciation of sophisticated weapons that now characterized the battlefield.

The Egyptian operational plan in the Sinai was called Operation *Kahir*, and until the last minute, Nasser tampered with it and changed it. This would result in considerable confusion when fighting broke out, and it contributed to a general lack of coordination at the launch of the campaign between senior and operational commanders, and between operational commanders and men in the field.

The Egyptian defense infrastructure was also known to be generally poor, and despite large numbers of combat aircraft, very few facilities such as underground revetments and hardened shelters, had been introduced to the main Egyptian Air Force bases. Electronic air defenses were also out of action, for reasons of internal security (Nasser did not trust his generals), which further opened up the skies for attack. Egyptian aircraft were most vulnerable on the ground, and it was there that the Israelis hit them.

Operation *Focus* (*Moked*) was launched at precisely 07h45 on Monday, June 5, 1967. The essence of the Israeli plan was simply to direct its entire air offensive capacity (just 12 aircraft were held back to defend Israeli airfields) to deal with Egyptian aircraft before the Syrians or the Jordanians had time to intervene, after which Israel would deal with each one in turn. Operation *Focus* was a highly coordinated, precisely timed series of attacks that initially targeted 10 Egyptian airfields in the first wave, and 9 more on the second. These attacks were intended to destroy the Egyptian Air Force while it was still on the ground.

The time of the first launch – 07h45 – was extremely important for four reasons. At that hour, the Egyptians had already flown their first morning combat patrols, so they were back on the ground at breakfast. Moreover, on a Monday morning, most Egyptian high ranking officers would either be at home or en route to work, taking them out of the picture during the vital moments of the attack. The timing also allowed the IAF pilots earmarked for the attack to enjoy a full night's sleep before the commencement of what would be a long and punishing day. Lastly, the normally heavy morning mist and fog over the combat zone would have lifted by then, allowing for better target acquisition.

The initial attack lasted 80 minutes, comprising eight waves of four aircraft each. The planes spent about 10 minutes over the target area, followed typically less than three minutes later by the next. After the initial 80 minute assault, the Egyptians were given just 10 minutes to catch their breath before the second 80 minute attack was launched. By noon, a total of 19 Egyptian airfields had been comprehensively targeted in the Sinai, the Suez Canal Zone, in and around Cairo, up the Nile Valley, and on the west bank of the Red Sea. In those first three hours, the Egyptian Air Force lost 300 of its 340 aircraft, including its entire fleet of Soviet-supplied TU-16 long-range bombers and almost all of its combat aircraft.

A picture of destroyed Egyptian planes on the ground

Israeli intelligence was also able to pinpoint only operationally significant targets, which avoided wasted time, while finely rehearsed turnarounds of 10-12 minutes ensured that Israeli aircraft were applied to maximum effect.

In Damascus and Amman, the Syrians and Jordanians, although immediately appraised of the launch of Operation *Focus*, failed to launch any sort of response of their own, allowing the IAF to demolish the Egyptians and then immediately afterwards move to destroy both the Syrian and Jordanian air forces on the ground. The Syrians lost 60 of their 90 aircraft, while the Jordanian Air Force was entirely obliterated.

Thus, by mid-afternoon on June 5, the very first day of the war, Israel had achieved unchallenged air supremacy over all three fronts. This offered complete freedom of movement to operational commanders, after which a majority of Israeli strike aircraft could undertake ground support operations.

The land war followed the air war very quickly and was also launched first against Egyptian forces in the Sinai. On the eve of war, the Egyptians had moved a total of five infantry divisions and two armored divisions into the Sinai, comprising a force of some 170,000 troops (100,000 front line troops), 1,000 tanks, 1,100 APCs and 1,000 artillery pieces, along with hundreds of mixed artillery pieces. Generally, however, the Egyptian deployment was defensive, in keeping with Soviet doctrine, with infantry placed forward along the presumed line of Israeli advance, and with heavy armor and artillery deployed to the rear in a fortified framework utilizing strategic depth. The Egyptians obviously anticipated a circling maneuver south, where most of their force was concentrated, and the notion of a full frontal attack directly through their center seems never to have occurred to them.

Strategic depth, in the meanwhile, also defined the Israeli operational doctrine. The Sinai Peninsula, effectively a militarized zone occupied mostly by nomadic Bedouins, offered a territorial buffer to whichever side controlled it. The aim of Israel, therefore, was to use the opportunity now provided to gain the improved national security that its original borders lacked. Into this theatre, therefore, Israel placed the comparative heavy force of three divisions, each of about 15,000 men, 300 tanks and various artillery pieces.

Israeli commander, General Ariel Sharon, remarked once that tank battles are battles for roads, and moving to control all of the few roads and junctions that traverse the Sinai was the first Israeli objective. Initially, the Egyptians held all of the key roads and junctions throughout the region, and these were protected by massed defensive formations and with the dispersal of fortified positions, anticipating that the Israelis would themselves be forced to disperse, thus diminishing their strength. The Israeli commanders, however, took a different view. They recognized the need for a short, decisive, violent and above all, winnable war. Israel's lack of numbers, its reliance on a citizen's army, and its inability to sustain a heavy loss of life all demanded this. To engage a numerically superior force in a full-frontal fight would ultimately have been suicidal. The essence of the Israeli strategy, therefore, was maneuver, hoping to keep casualties to a minimum and win a quick, decisive victory.

Sharon during the war

The Israeli plan, therefore, required a three-phase attack, with the first phase being a three-pronged breakthrough initiated from Israel's border with the Sinai. One division would enter the Sinai in the area of Khan Yunis, south of Gaza, a second would penetrate towards an important road junction called Abu Ageila, about 15 miles into the Sinai, and about 25 miles south of the Mediterranean coast while a third division would drive between the two, over a landscape of dunes that the Egyptians had calculated was impassable to tracked vehicles. In all three cases, the emphasis was on tank maneuver under the protection of air interdiction, with a minimal emphasis on infantry and artillery in support roles.

By June 6, the Egyptians had been pushed back, with their strategy of static defense largely ineffective against the rapid and agile Israeli deployments. In the face of massed tanks and artillery, the Israeli armored brigades often simply bypassed Egyptian positions, moving to secure the key passes in the central Sinai, particularly the Mitla and Gidi Passes, through which the Egyptians would be forced to retreat. Then, quickly reforming ahead of the Egyptian line of retreat, and after effectively severing their lines of communication, the Egyptians suddenly found themselves trapped in a killing field between advancing and blocking Israeli forces. Over the course of the next few days, as the Israelis grew in confidence, and as Egyptian resistance in the Sinai collapsed, the front-line retracted steadily west towards the Suez Canal.

The Israeli columns began very quickly to stretch their own supply lines and to challenge logistics. In advance of this likelihood, several Egyptian airbases had been occupied and repurposed by the Israelis to airlift in fuel, ammunition, and supplies.

As this was going on, a United Nations ceasefire in the Sinai was debated in anguished emergency sessions of the Security Council. The Israelis obfuscated and delayed as much as possible, as did General Nasser, but a ceasefire did ultimately come into effect at 04h35 on June 9, 1967. By then, the Israelis had conquered and occupied the entire Sinai Peninsula east of the Suez Canal. Egyptian losses in what proved to be a disastrous campaign were estimated at 12,000 men and 700 tanks, while the Israelis suffered the loss of 275 troops and 61 tanks. A more definitive victory could hardly have been hoped for.

The Sinai campaign of 1967 is generally regarded as one of the greatest tank engagements in the history of mechanized warfare, though the Egyptian misuse of tanks has also on occasions been cited as a factor in Israel's victory. The Soviet tank doctrine of the time placed a greater emphasis on the use of tanks as field artillery pieces, placed in a static formation and used in principle to destroy advancing enemy armor by the use of accurate fire from fixed positions. This, however, was very adroitly countered by Israeli agility, and the ability of IDF columns to hit the Egyptians on the flank and cut off their rear, all while enjoying the cover of air support against tightly packed and immobile Egyptian formations.

A picture of Israeli tanks drilling before the war

The 1967 war also demonstrated Israeli cohesion on the field of battle. The Israeli army was built largely on the British model, and all service commanders served in the General

Headquarters under the Chief-of-Staff, who in this case was the respected Israeli General Yitzak Rabin. Three sectoral commands – north, south and central – were also part of GHQ. Southern Command, headed by Brigadier General Yeshayahu Gavish, enjoyed the involvement of three gifted operational commanders: Brigadier General Yisrael Tal, Brigadier General Avraham Yoffe and Brigadier General Ariel Sharon, each commanding what in Israeli military parlance was known as an *Ugdah*. This was a tactical task force, essentially a division configured for a specific, assigned mission. All three tactical commanders reported to the sectoral command, Brigadier General Gavish, but were also capable of high levels of autonomous action, and while they were bound by the common objective of destroying the Egyptians and taking the Sinai, they were each tasked with different objectives. Unity of effort, however, was intrinsic, not only in part because of a common investment in the outcome, but also because of exhaustive preparation and training in the pre-war planning and exercise phase.

Rabin

This contrasted sharply with clear deficits in the Egyptian command structure. The most obvious feature of this was the tight control exercised by General Nasser himself, sitting upon a top-heavy higher command, and a rather loosely configured and ill-defined sectoral command. Force integration, coordination, and general unity of command and effort did not really exist in the Egyptian defense establishment. Operation *Kahir* as a broad operational strategy had been on the table for some time – mobile defense as a means of drawing the Israeli's into the peninsular to be enveloped and crushed – but the plan was never articulated beyond the boardroom commanders, and certainly, it was never drilled and exercised on a tactical level.

Nasser, at the last minute, also altered the fundamental elements of the plan to avoid, for political reasons, any incursion by the Israelis into Egyptian territory. Therefore, the concept of drawing the Israelis into battle in the Sinai, and there dispersing and crushing them, meant nothing. Now it was imperative to keep the Israelis out of Egypt altogether, and so a static defense was adopted to stop the Israeli's in their tracks. Few, if any field commanders knew about this, however, and as the Israeli attack was being rolled out, many senior Egyptian commanders were absent from the field. As the Israelis had anticipated, on the morning of June 5, they were commuting through traffic on their way to work.

Another point of comparison between the two armies is that of intelligence. By 1967, Israeli intelligence had achieved the status of being one of the most admired in the world. With the nation in a situation whereby its major cities lay minutes away from enemy airfields, accurate intelligence probably impacted Israeli national security more than any other nation on earth. The gathering and dissemination of Israeli intelligence in the opening air attack was faultless, and although its effectiveness varied in other phases of the Sinai campaign, it certainly marked a cornerstone of the Israeli victory.

Egyptian intelligence, on the other hand, was virtually non-existent. Nasser went ahead with his verbal war against Israel with no clear idea of what he was up against. Arguably the single biggest failure of Egyptian intelligence was the abject underestimation of Israeli Air Force capability, for which the Egyptian Air Force paid with its very existence.

Jordan

By the afternoon of June 5, with the Egyptian Air Force in ruins, and Egyptian land forces on the run in the Sinai, the IDF turned its attention to the West Bank. Jordan had been partitioned from the British Mandate of Palestine and given to the Hashemite monarchy of Saudi Arabia, so it was never really held as an equal partner in the anti-Israeli Arab brotherhood. Despite Hashemite rule, the West Bank, and what came to be known as Transjordan, was in practical terms a Palestinian nation, with its government and civil service largely Palestinian, along with which came inevitable Palestinian aspirations to own Jordan as the coveted Palestinian state. Jordan, therefore, so long as no inconvenient mutual defense pacts came into effect, was not anticipated by the Israelis to present much of a military problem. The entirety of Jordanian armed forces comprised just eight infantry brigades and two armored brigades, a total of perhaps 56,000 men, and 287 tanks. Nonetheless, the initial Israeli preference was for a defensive posture against Jordan, with the emphasis then on action in the Sinai and the Golan.

Israeli Prime Minister Eshkol sent a message to Jordanian leader King Hussein, via Norwegian General Odd Bull, Chief of Staff of the United Nations Truce Supervision Organization (UNTSO), offering an assurance that no hostile action would be initiated against Jordan if Jordan stayed out of the war. Nasser, in the confusion that followed the initial air attacks against Egypt, was able, however, to convince King Hussein that Egypt had been victorious in those initial encounters and that a flight of aircraft visible on radar was an Egyptian squadron en route to bomb Tel Aviv.[2]

King Hussein was taken in, and at 09h45 on the morning of June 5, the Jordanian army opened an artillery barrage against Jerusalem and Jewish communities on the border. Shells also fell on the suburbs of Tel Aviv, illustrating once again Israel's fundamental vulnerability to outside attack. By 11h15, Jordanian artillery began to range west Jerusalem, eventually targeting the Prime Minister's residence, various military installations, and the Knesset building. Jordanian ground troops then moved in and took over the abandoned United Nations base of Armon Hanatziv on the eastern outskirts of Jerusalem. At 11h50, a squadron of 16 Jordanian Hawker

---

[2] The aircraft were in fact Israel fighters returning from a sortie over Egypt.

Hunters hit targets in northern Israel, followed by three Iraqi Hawker Hunters and a Tu-16 bomber which was shot down near the Megiddo Airfield.

The Jordanian action, ill-informed as it was, nonetheless offered the opportunity for Israel to fulfill the most cherished objective of its existence so far: the reunification of Jerusalem under Israeli control. This was not cited as an objective, and numerous public messages from commanders and politicians forswore it, but such was the Israeli yearning for a return to the Old City that everyone was thinking about it.

King Hussein ultimately realized his error too late. Israeli jets began hitting targets in Jordan, Syria, and Iraq shortly after 12h30 on June 5. In short order, the Jordanian Air Force no longer existed, while on the tarmacs in various Syrian airbases, some 50 combat aircraft lay burning. The Iraqis similarly lost 10 combat aircraft shot down. One Israeli jet was shot down by ground fire, and other strategic targets and troop movements in both territories were also hit.

So rapidly had matters advanced that an emergency cabinet meeting was convened to consider all of these developments. A strong lobby of military and civil figures on the right argued for the launch of an immediate action to take East Jerusalem. Prime Minister Eshkol, however, was reluctant, for obvious political reasons, so he deferred the matter to his Minister of Defense, Moshe Dayan, and his Chief-of-Staff, Yitzhak Rabin. Dayan, often seen to be hesitant at crucial moments, demurred, allowing only limited retaliatory action for the time being.

By mid-afternoon, however, Jordanian troops had moved in to occupy a key position in the north of the city known as Ammunition Hill, and Government House, an international zone that was the headquarters of the UN observation force. They also held pockets all over the Old City. Clearly, the Jordanians were keen to make a fight of it, and hold their positions. That night, Eshkol relented and ordered an Israeli offensive to retake Government House, beginning a fierce overnight encounter that is now celebrated as the Battle of Ammunition Hill. Fighting began in the early hours of June 6, commencing with an artillery barrage and concluding in a paratroop and infantry assault sent in at 06h30 that morning. 36 Israeli soldiers and 71 Jordanians were killed in the action, and many more injured, but the Jordanians were removed, and the Israelis took over the two positions.

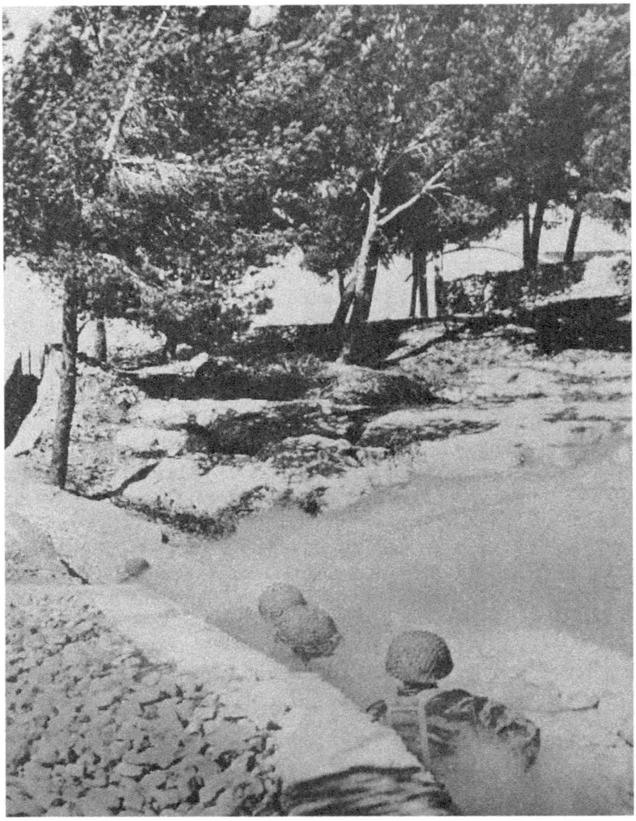

Pictures of Israeli paratroopers during the battle

Elsewhere in East Jerusalem, fierce fighting was underway as the Israelis moved to encircle the city and dislodge dug-in and fortified Jordanian positions, including the Police Academy and, of course, the UN position at Ammunition Hill. By mid-morning on June 6, Mount Scopus and the campus of the Hebrew University was in Israeli hands, followed soon afterwards by the American Colony.[3]

From the American Colony, Israeli troops probed deeper into the Old City, but they were ordered by Dayan not to enter. This was done out of respect for interfaith holy sites, and to run no risk of damaging them, but Dayan also worried about the potential of an international reaction if Israeli forces muscled their way into those very holy sites. Dayan was perhaps also mindful of the possibility that having won the prize of East Jerusalem, Israel might then be forced to relinquish it under the threat of international sanctions.

---

[3] *The American Colony* was an American Christian utopian society established in Jerusalem in the 1880s, which by 1967 had been converted into a hotel although the district remained known as the American Colony.

However, on June 7, he abruptly changed his mind. Without cabinet clearance, and in a rather uncharacteristically determined mood, he ordered Israeli troops to move in quickly and take the Old City. The operation was mounted almost entirely by paratroop brigades, utilizing no tanks or artillery for fear of damaging holy sites, but by then, in any case, Jordanian resistance was beginning to crumble. By noon, the brigade commander was able to report over his two-way radio the occupation of the Temple Mount. The Israeli flag was hoisted alongside the Western Wall, where religious services were read that evening.[4] Later, Prime Minister Eshkol, Defense Minister Dayan and the Chief of General Staff, Lieutenant General Rabin, arrived in the city to witness the historic moment themselves. It was the first time in nearly 20 years Jews had been allowed at their holiest site.

No specific orders were given to advance the occupation of the west bank beyond East Jerusalem, but when intelligence reports were received indicating that King Hussein had ordered the withdrawal of Jordanian and Iraqi forces east of the Jordan River, Dayan issued the order for Israeli troops to effectively occupy all of the territories west of the Jordan River.

Syria

Israeli tanks in the Golan

The third major front of the Six Day War was the Golan Heights, one of the most strategically important positions in the region. Located on the northern border of Israel, it was occupied by Syria. The Golan Heights is defined by a shallow plateau of land lying at an average height of 3,300 feet, and located on the southern lee of Mount Hermon. It overlooks the Jordan Valley, the Hula Valley and Galilee, and in 1967, it threatened most of northern Israel. It was then, as it remains, a superb defensive position, protecting the Israeli approaches to Damascus. The positions were occupied by 40,000 Syrian troops, 260 tanks, and artillery placements built to a depth of 10 miles.

The IAF had already dealt with the Syrian Air Force, so Israeli air interdiction against Syrian

---

[4] Jews had been for the most part denied access to Jewish religious sites in the Old City while East Jerusalem lay under de facto Jordanian annexation.

positions on the Golan were largely unopposed. The bulk of the IDF, however, was still busy dealing with the Egyptians in the Sinai, and others were fighting in East Jerusalem, so the Israeli cabinet met to consider how best to move forward on the Golan, or whether to move at all.

There were ticklish political and military problems peculiar to the Golan Heights that had not complicated operations elsewhere. The Golan Heights, for example, unlike the Sinai and the West Bank, was indisputably Syrian territory. To occupy it would transgress international law in a manner that could not be obfuscated by incomplete treaties and broken agreements, as so much of Israel proper could be. But nonetheless, so long as they held the Golan, the Syrians held a Sword of Damocles over Israel that could not be ignored. The Syrians were certainly guilty of encouraging the PLO and other groups in attacks against Israel from its territory, and periodic tank and artillery duels rocked the front lines. In the end, for the Israelis, taking the Golan would prove to be too tempting.

Dayan, however, for a few days at least, opposed plans for Israel to attack the Golan, not only for fear of Soviet intervention if Syrian casualties became too heavy, but also because the simple logistical challenge of storming the heights from the Jordan Valley would be both difficult and costly in lives and armor. According to the minutes of the Knesset Foreign Affairs and Defense Committee, released to the State Archive early in 2017, Dayan's exact words on the matter were as follows: "We started the war to root out the Egyptian force and open the straits [of Tiran]. On the way, we took the whole West Bank. I don't think that meanwhile, we can start another battle, with the Syrians. If that is the question, I'd vote against it. If we're going into Syria to change the border to make it easier for the farms [in the Hula Valley], because the Syrians are shooting at them, I'd be against it."

Dayan argued that, with the limited forces currently available to Northern Command, the Israelis would probably be capable only of securing the first line of Syrian positions overlooking the Hula Valley (Israel's principal agricultural region), which would not really aid Israeli farmers who were under constant threat of Syrian barrage.

Opposing Dayan was Northern Command and the Prime Minister, who were more open to the idea of an attack, and by June 9, Dayan had changed his mind. Part of the reason for this, it has been suggested, is the interpretation of aerial photographs passed on to him by the Directorate of Military Intelligence. These presented an unexpected picture of Syrian deployments on the Golan Heights, particularly in the city of Quneitra, where the Syrian sectoral military HQ was located. What had a day or two earlier been a landscape teeming with military activity was now largely empty. The question, of course, was whether Syrian resistance on the Golan, subject to heavy aerial interdiction and artillery assault, had collapsed, or whether Syrian forces had simply moved closer to the front.

At more or less the same time, as Israeli forces began to arrive on the east bank of the Suez Canal, an absolute Egyptian defeat became increasingly difficult for General Nasser to deny. Word began to circulate back to the Israeli high command that the Egyptian president was mulling over the terms of a UN-brokered ceasefire and urging Syria to do the same.[5] Dayan was then persuaded; troops and equipment from the Sinai were now becoming available to support operations in Syria, and Northern Command was ordered to move.[6]

---

[5] At the onset of fighting, Nasser maintained the determined position that Egyptian forces were victorious, and that the Israelis had been crushed. This he allowed to influence the decisions of his alliance partners, in particular Jordan, which acted on assurances from Egypt that the Israeli southern front had collapsed. Nasser's deputy, and future Egyptian president Anwar Sadat, entering military headquarters in Cairo at 11h00 on June 5, hours into the war, noted: *"I just went home and stayed in for days... unable to watch the crowds... chanting, dancing, and applauding the faked-up victory reports which our mass media put out hourly."*

[6] McGeorge Bundy, the US National Security Adviser, spoke obliquely to Israeli Foreign Minister Abba Eban on the question of an Israeli attack

On the morning of June 9, the Israeli Air Force commenced heavy bombing operations against Syrian positions on the Banias plateau, Tel Hamra and Tel Azaziyat, and by noon, units of the Northern Command, headed by Major General David Elazar, had crossed the armistice line and were moving into Syrian territory. Elazar decided to break through at as many points as possible, choosing the northern sector of the Golan, flanked by Mount Hermon, because it was both the most difficult terrain to mount such an operation, and because as such it was the most lightly defended. The main trunk road crossing the Golan also lay in this quarter, and with control of that road, the Israelis would be in a position to attack the Syrian front line from the rear. From there, Israeli forces would move towards the center of the Golan plateau, occupying the key Syrian town of Quneitra, through which passed the road to the Syrian capital of Damascus.

By 18h30 on June 10, the day after the land operation began, a United Nations ceasefire came into effect. Israel had taken occupation of the southwest portion of Syria, from the Golan to within 40 miles of Damascus. Syrian forces were on the run, and Soviet saber rattling began to be heard as a complete Syrian defeat became inevitable. The Americans, and by extension the Israelis, were warned to go no further. This victory came at a cost of 115 Israeli soldiers and 2,500 Syrians, with each side losing 100 and 120 tanks respectively.

That day, the war was ended by the negotiation of a ceasefire, as all sides had anticipated. The Israelis, for obvious reasons, were the least interested in an early ceasefire, and Israeli diplomats fought a parallel war in the United Nations Security Council to deflect the question until Israeli objectives had been achieved. These, of course, were territorial and pivoted almost entirely on the need for strategic depth.

The process began on the evening of June 6, when a draft resolution was passed which was accepted by Israel and Jordan but rejected by Egypt, Syria and Iraq. This became the pattern, and it was not until day three of the war, as Israel began to make territorial advances in East Jerusalem, that the Jordanians began to plead with the United States and the United Nations to pressure Israel to cease and desist. This was the first sign of real pain from the Arab coalition. This time the Israelis demurred, and indeed, it was the very potential for a ceasefire that prompted the Israelis to move with dispatch on East Jerusalem in order to gain control of it before any ceasefire could come into effect.

Until the end of day four of the war, Nasser maintained the fiction that his forces were victorious, but as the Israelis approached the Suez Canal, and the destruction of his army could no longer be denied, he abruptly ordered the Egyptian ambassador to the United Nations to accept the terms of the ceasefire. Syria followed suit the next day, June 9. A ceasefire on the Golan went into effect on June 10.

The Aftermath

"We have unified Jerusalem, the divided capital of Israel. We have returned to the holiest of our Holy Places, never to depart from it again." – Moshe Dayan

The war in 1967 was, without a doubt, the finest hour of the Israeli military establishment and the IDF. The cost of operations, in lives and materiel, was heavy, but victory was absolute and comprehensive, and all of Israel's strategic objectives had been achieved. The Arab armies had once again been humiliated, and there began to take root in Israel a feeling that this was indeed the key moment in Israel's journey towards fulfillment. It began to be widely believed that while future generations of Arabs might make threats, they would never join in battle with Israel again.

---

on the Golan, remarking as follows: *"Bundy went on to reflect, in a tentative voice, that it would seem strange that Syria – which had originated the war – might be the only one that seemed to be getting off without injury. Might it not turn out, paradoxically, he said, that less guilty Arab states, such as Jordan, had suffered heavy loss, while Syria would be free to start the whole deadly sequence again."*

The Israelis won a smashing victory for a number of reasons. Perhaps most notably, the Israelis were expecting war, and they had no doubt that war was pending, not only because of Nasser's belligerence but also because of the threats made by other key Arab leaders. Arab planning, or perhaps more accurately lack of planning, was advertised reasonably freely, and a complete lack of unity of command and purpose between the three main belligerents simply confirmed this fact. No single Arab partner fought within an integrated command, which Israeli intelligence understood completely, and so the Israelis were able to deal with each one in turn without significant interference from the other. This was particularly the case during the first waves of air assaults.

Expecting war, therefore, the Israelis were in a position to prepare for it, and perhaps their greatest achievement was the complete and absolute surprise suffered by the Arabs as the Israelis went into action. If a preemptive strike was desired, then the Israelis achieved it on a spectacular level. Initial deception involved the mounting of several large air patrols south towards the Gulf of Aqaba, convincing the Egyptians that the Israeli main effort would be focused there, and many Egyptian front line units were shifted south in anticipation of this.

Thus, when the attack came, it was from a wholly unexpected direction. Israeli aircraft came in from the west, circling far out into the Mediterranean, and not from the north or the east as might be expected. So unexpected was this, indeed, that the Egyptians were convinced that American or British aircraft carriers had somehow been involved in the operation.

Israeli land operations were also characterized by feint and deception, and troop build-ups and dispositions caused the Egyptians to deploy south, never expecting the full frontal assault west through the center of the Sinai. To an extent, the Golan operation was also carefully stage-managed to present a deception. There was little alternative but to approach the Golan Heights from the west, but focusing the breakthrough where the terrain was hardest to manage was successful in catching the Syrians off balance.

Accurate and timely intelligence, well-analyzed and effectively distributed, was arguably Israel's most effective weapon. The imperative of surviving a very precarious early history had bred in the Israeli security establishment a deep reliance on good intelligence. Israeli pilots knew precisely what they were looking for, knew where enemy combat aircraft were located, and knew how to avoid radar and detection. The operation was clinically managed, somewhat unlike the usual Israeli preference for operational simplicity, but it was so well-rehearsed and drilled that it ran like clockwork.

Operational security was another Israeli achievement. Arab operational plans leaked like a sieve, and it's possible the free dissemination of information was intended ultimately to intimidate the Israelis. Israeli operational security, on the other hand, was deployed from the top down. When Prime Minister Eshkol decided to proceed with the war, the date of the launch was given to Dayan to decide, and it was he who communicated it to operational command. The Arabs, the Americans, and the Soviets all had no idea that Israel was about to go to war.

Through maneuver, simplicity, economy of force, objective, and unity of command, the Israeli military achievement in 1967 was a textbook example of a clinical war fought for quick results with a clear sense of purpose. National survival was the first objective, and security in the future was the second. Both were achieved, with the added benefit of an almost total destruction of Arab offensive capability, not to mention the moral satisfaction of having given them an unholy beating.

Speaking three weeks after the war had ended, as he accepted an honorary degree from Hebrew University, Rabin gave his reasoning behind the success of Israel: "Our airmen, who struck the enemies' planes so accurately that no one in the world understands how it was done and people seek technological explanations or secret weapons; our armored troops who beat the enemy even when their equipment was inferior to his; our soldiers in all other branches…who overcame our enemies everywhere, despite the latter's superior numbers and fortifications—all these revealed not only coolness and courage in the battle but…an understanding that only their personal stand against the greatest dangers would achieve victory for their country and for their families, and that if victory was not theirs the alternative was annihilation."

Israeli sovereignty over Jerusalem marked the moment of the Jews' return to some of the most important religious sites of the faith. The power of this symbol can hardly be overstated, but it naturally provoked dismay throughout the Islamic world. Nonetheless, the Israeli government was quick to reassure Christians and Muslims that their religious freedoms would be respected. On June 27, the Knesset passed three laws:

1) Empowering the government to extend Israeli law and administration to all parts of Eretz Yisrael.

2) Authorizing the interior minister to extend the jurisdiction of Israeli municipalities to parts of the area.

3) Providing penalties of up to seven years' imprisonment for the desecration of Holy Places, or barring any person from free access to the Holy Places of his religion.

At the beginning of July, a representative of the Vatican, Monsignor Angelo Felici, visited Israel, and various vague and placatory statements were issued by him and the Israelis. In general, an attempt was made to frame the reunification of the city under Israeli administration as an advantage to all. A representative of United Nations Secretary-General, U Thant, paid a visit in August, and he too described himself as encouraged, offering the impression that the city seemed peaceful and orderly. The local PLO leadership expressed its opposition to Israeli rule, which was to be expected.

Jerusalem was a fait accompli, but in regard to the other occupied territories, there was for the most part unanimous international disapproval. As a consequence of these conquests, Israel magnified its territorial holdings several times and added a large population to its responsibility. The Sinai was of little practical consequence other than as strategic depth in regard to Israeli security, and without significant guarantees from the Arab alliance, there was little hope in the short term of the Sinai being returned to Egypt.

Likewise, the Golan, once in Israeli hands, was simply too valuable to relinquish. The West Bank and Gaza, on the other hands, were significant for the expansion of Jews out of Israel in the first instance, and the large refugee population of Palestinians in the second.

On August 29, 1967, an Arab League Summit was held in the Sudanese capital of Khartoum, and there the Arab response to the events of the summer was discussed. The meeting was attended by 8 Arab heads of state: Egypt, Syria, Jordan, Lebanon, Iraq, Algeria, Kuwait, and Sudan. From this conference came the Khartoum Resolution, listing the three "Nos." These were no peace with Israel, no recognition of Israel, and no negotiations with Israel.

Months later, on November 22, 1967, the United Nations Security Council passed Resolution 242, still one of the central resolutions of the conflict. Creating the "land for peace" formula, the resolution called for "[t]ermination of all claims or states of belligerency and respect for and acknowledgment of the sovereignty, territorial integrity and political independence of every State in the area and their right to live in peace within secure and recognized boundaries free from threats or acts of force."

In exchange for the Arab nations ending their belligerency and acknowledging Israel's sovereignty, Resolution 242 called for the "[w]ithdrawal of Israel armed forces from territories occupied in the recent conflict." This is one of the most important and most misunderstood aspects of the resolution. Although a simple reading of the language seems to call upon Israel to return to the Green Line and give back all of the lands captured during the Six Day War, the U.N. diplomats did not intend for that. The language intentionally left out the word "the" in front of the word territories, an indication that the resolution did not call upon Israel to return to the Green Line before the Six Day War of 1967.

Resolution 242 was drafted by the British, whose U.N. Ambassador, Lord Caradon, later said, "It would have been wrong to demand that Israel return to its positions of June 4, 1967, because those positions were undesirable and artificial. After all, they were just the places where the soldiers of each side happened to be on the day the fighting stopped in 1948. They were just armistice lines. That's why we didn't demand that the Israelis return to them." Similarly, the American U.N. Ambassador said, "The notable omissions – which were not accidental – in regard to withdrawal are the words "the" or "all" and the "June 5, 1967 lines" ... the resolution speaks of withdrawal from occupied territories without defining the extent of withdrawal... Israel's prior frontiers had proved to be notably Insecure."

At the time, the Israelis made contingent any return of captured territory on peace, and this was backed up by the United States. President Johnson spoke out against any permanent change in the legal and political status of the Israeli-occupied territories and emphasized that Arab land should be returned only as part of an overall peace settlement that recognized Israel's right to exist.

In the wake of the war, the Israeli establishment was fully expecting the Arabs to capitulate, sue for peace, and deal with Israel over the fundamentals of Israeli existence. Defense Minister Moshe Dayan made the now famous comment that he was "waiting for a telephone call" from the Arabs, but that call never came. Within a few weeks, instead, what came to be known as the War of Attrition began along the Suez. General Nasser, unable to find a solution to the Israeli problem, and now effectively disarmed, adopted a policy of low-level war along the Suez Canal, which Dayan referred to as the best tank ditch in the world. This settled into regular tank and artillery duels over the next six years, with occasional air raids and periodic commando operations. No peace with Israel was contemplated in Egypt.

Superpower Involvement in the Six Day War

"Certainly, troops must be withdrawn; but there must also be recognized rights of national life, progress in solving the refugee problem, freedom of innocent maritime passage, limitation of the arms race, and respect for political independence and territorial integrity." – President Johnson

By the late 1960s, the Cold War was at its peak. Israel had always been part of the Western camp, while the Arab states, particularly Egypt and Syria, were aligned to various degrees with the Soviet Union. Jordan was the exception to this, and King Hussein, although clearly allied to the West, maintained a non-aligned position, citing his opposition to communist atheism and his support of the freedom of Arab nationalist aspirations to develop apart from any form of imperialist influence from either side.

Nasser, as the voice of Arab nationalism and international anti-imperialism, was the poster child for Soviet engagement in the Arab world, and this would remain the case until his death in 1970. His successor, Anwar Sadat, would be the architect of the Yom Kippur War in 1973, but he was also responsible for steering Egypt towards the American sphere of influence, where it remained for the balance of the Cold War.

The Six Day War, however, was seen as a failure on the part of the administrations of Eisenhower, Kennedy and Johnson to prevent conflict in the Middle East in the aftermath of the 1956 Suez Crisis. At the same time, the situation presented the first real opportunity since the creation of Israel to establish the basis of a lasting and stable political solution in the region. Prior to 1967, the United States had held itself bound to what was known as the Tripartite Alliance, which was, in essence, a British initiative that included France and the United States and aimed to control aggression in the Middle East through the controlled sale of arms.

The United States had pressed Israel to withdraw from the Sinai Peninsula and Gaza Strip after the Suez Canal Crisis in 1956, and it had rejected Israeli requests for all but limited quantities of defensive weapons. By the time Johnson took office, however, unregulated Soviet arms supplies to Arab countries had begun to erode Israeli military superiority, which presented the potential for a preemptive strike, or even the development of Israeli nuclear weapons. The sale of U.S. arms to Israel increased, under the classic arms-race rationale that neither side could win.

Then, just as the threat of conventional war began to diminish, the rise of Palestinian terror groups established a new pattern of conflict, and proxy support for these movements by Israel's Arab neighbors set the tone for war in the region once again.

With the Egyptian blockade of the Gulf of Aqaba, Johnson attempted a lackluster enforcement of international law by proposing Operation *Red Sea Regatta*, but the effort failed to get off the ground, and the State Department then fell back on appeal-diplomacy, pressing the Soviets to apply pressure on Nasser while the U.S. itself applied pressure on Israel. In the end, the Johnson administration took the view that if the Israelis wanted to go it alone, then they might do so, and in the end, this would probably best serve the long-term interests of the United States in the region.

The Soviets, on the other hand, took a somewhat more aggressive position. They had supplied the Arab states with most of their arms, and it was the Soviets who circulated the original false intelligence that the Israelis were massing and preparing for war. It was also the Black Sea Fleet's appearance in the Red Sea that added teeth to Nasser's closing of the Straits of Tiran. The Soviet military command persuaded its political leadership to support these steps, knowing that they were intended to start a war to destroy Israel.

On June 5, after the launch of the Israeli pre-emptive strike, Soviet Prime Minister Alexei Kosygin made the first use of a hotline to Washington that had been installed following the Cuban missile crisis of 1962. "A very crucial moment has now arrived," he said. "Which forces us, if military actions are not stopped in the next few hours, to adopt an independent decision. We are ready to do this. However, these actions may bring us into a clash which will lead to a grave catastrophe...we purpose [sic] that you demand from Israel that it unconditionally cease military action...we purpose [sic] to warn Israel that if this is not fulfilled, necessary actions will be taken, including military."

This was fighting talk, but at the time, Johnson and his political advisors did not take it entirely seriously. In subsequent years, however, as records have come to light, it is clear that the Soviets were serious, and that advanced plans to invade Israel and avoid a total Israeli victory were indeed on the table. These initially took the form of an ad hoc "volunteer" landing force that would have been overcome by the Israelis, but not without cost, and it certainly would have globalized the conflict, bringing in the United States on some level.

The Israelis, while likely not aware of the specifics of all of this, discussed the potential for direct Soviet action, especially as the weight of victory began to swing so conspicuously in their favor. No unusual contingencies were made, however, and no early warning was received.

A point also worth noting is that during the war, Israeli aircraft and torpedo boats attacked a U.S. Navy technical research ship, the USS *Liberty*, operating in the eastern Mediterranean. The attack was put down as a friendly fire incident, but 34 American crew members, two Marines, and one civilian were killed. Some have suggested that the ship was deliberately targeted to prevent its intelligence gathering capability from benefiting the Egyptians. This is unlikely, and the truth is probably that the attack was accidental, but it certainly served the dual role of preventing covert Soviet plans from being discovered.

Pictures of the USS *Liberty* after the attack

In a 1993 interview for the Johnson Presidential Library oral history archives, U.S. Secretary of Defense Robert McNamara revealed that the U.S. Sixth Fleet, on a training exercise near Gibraltar, was re-positioned towards the eastern Mediterranean to be able to defend Israel. Nasser's appeals in the first hours of the war that Israeli air attacks must have originated from U.S. or British carriers was in part seen to be substantiated by the presence in the Mediterranean of the U.S. Sixth Fleet. "President Johnson and I," Robert McNamara added in the interview cited above, "decided to turn the fleet around and send it back toward Israel, not to join with Israel in an attack on Syria - not at all - but to be close enough to Israel so, if the Soviets supported a Syrian attack on Israel, we could come to Israel's defense with the fleet, prevent Israel from being annihilated."

The Soviet task force, however, never landed. Brinkmanship might have accounted for this, but soon afterwards the Soviet Union severed diplomatic relations with Israel. Soviet credibility was somewhat tarnished as a consequence of this, but even more so by the ease with which the Israelis had been able to defeat a formidable alliance of enemies, all armed with the best that Soviet arms manufacturers could provide, not to mention the expertise of thousands of Soviet military advisers. Soon enough, President Kosygin found himself having to reassure numerous proxies, Cuban leader Fidel Castro among them, that Soviet support could be relied upon. The Soviet failure to support the Arabs in their defeat had simply been due to Arab confidence that victory could be achieved upon their own resources, which clearly proved not to be the case.

Ultimately, the United States and other Western allies supported Resolution 242 in its essential elements but held out for Arab reciprocation in the various security guarantees and acknowledgement of Israel's right to exist. The Khartoum Declaration of 1967 confirmed than no such acknowledgement would occur, which left open the possibility for Israel to indefinitely retain occupation of the conquered territories, and also the inevitably of at least one more major war.

The Occupied Territories

Peace for us means the destruction of Israel. We are preparing for an all-out war, a war which will last for generations – Yasser Arafat

The term "Occupied Territories" was first used in the United Nations Resolution 242, and it has since come to form part of the established political lexicon of the Middle East. According to a post-war census, just under 1 million additional people came under Israeli administration as a consequence of the territorial conquests of the Six Day War. These were scattered unevenly through northern Sinai (the only populated regions of the Sinai existed along the coast, since Bedouin populations tended to exist outside formal administration of any sort), the Golan Heights, the Gaza Strip, and the West Bank.

The Sinai very quickly came under military administration as part of the Israeli Military Governorate (1967–1981/1982) and remained in practical terms a militarized zone. The Israelis established a sectoral military command for the Sinai, and the only regular Israeli tank battalion was permanently based there. A front line defense was established on the east bank of the Suez Canal, and the territorial occupation on either side remained unchanged and unchallenged until 1973, when Egypt launched what came to be known as the Yom Kippur War. Israel would remain in occupation of the Sinai until April 1982, when the last Israeli troops were withdrawn under the terms of a peace treaty signed with Egypt. After the Yom Kippur War, President Carter's administration sought to establish a peace process that would settle the conflict in the Middle East, while also reducing Soviet influence in the region. On September 17, 1978, after secret negotiations at the presidential retreat Camp David, Egyptian President Anwar Sadat and Israeli Prime Minister Menachem Begin signed a peace treaty between the two nations, in which Israel ceded the Sinai Peninsula to Egypt in exchange for a normalization of relations, making Egypt the first Arab adversary to officially recognize Israel. Carter also tried to create a peace process that would settle the rest of the conflict vis-à-vis the Israelis and Palestinians, but it never got off the ground. For the Camp David Accords, Begin and Sadat won the Nobel Peace Prize.

Begin had once been a leader of the paramilitary group Irgun, while Sadat had succeeded Nasser. The peace treaty cost Sadat his life, as he was assassinated in 1981 by fundamentalist military officers during a victory parade.

The Golan Heights, likewise, were quickly fortified and established as an Israeli defense buffer against Syria. Where once Syrian positions had overlooked the pastoral regions of the Hula Valley, now Israeli positions menaced the Quneitra Governorate of Syria. The Golan Heights also fell under the administration of the Israeli Military Governorate. Israel occupied about 500 square miles of the Golan Heights, from which a majority of Syrian civilians and non-combatants fled. Syria, as part of the Arab bloc, rejected the terms of the Resolution 242, so the Golan Heights remained substantively under Israeli military control until December 1981, when Israel formally annexed its portion of the Golan Heights, drawing it under the same formal civilian administration as the rest of Israel.[7]

Syria continued to demand a full Israeli withdrawal to the 1967 borders, including a strip of land on the east shore of the Sea of Galilee that Syria captured during the 1948 war that it occupied until 1967. Successive Israeli governments have considered an Israeli withdrawal from the Golan in return for normalization of relations with Syria, provided certain security concerns are met. Successive Syrian regimes have all rejected normalization with Israel, and the eruption of the Syrian Civil War has eliminated any discussion of such a withdrawal for the foreseeable future.

The West Bank, captured from Jordan, is probably the most important land that changed hands, at least form a political perspective. Nearly 600,000 Jordanians found themselves under Israeli military administration once the dust settled, of whom perhaps 60,000 were residents in 1948-era refugee camps. The region was something of a gray area in regard to how land and populations were distributed in the aftermath of the 1948 war. Originally designated Transjordan under the partition, it was an Ottoman territory that had always been regarded as part of Palestine, and since the majority of its Arab population claimed Palestinian origins, any Jordanian claim was disputable. The PLO remained recognized as the "sole legitimate representative of the Palestinian people," and in 1988, Jordan officially relinquished its claim to the region.[8]

In 1982, as part of the peace agreement between Israel and Egypt, the West Bank came under a semi-civil authority, which meant only that matters of Palestinian administration were dealt with by civilian officials in the Israeli Ministry of Defense. Israeli settlements, on the other hand, fell under Israeli civilian administration. Various international agreements and protocols would govern the direction and existence of the West Bank into a new era of Israeli politics, and even as Israeli occupation of the Golan and the Sinai would be challenged again in 1973, the West Bank remained firmly in Israeli hands.

At the end of the war, Israel took control of the heavily populated city of Gaza from Egypt, taking responsibility also for 356,000 people, of whom 175,000 were in refugee camps. Prior to the Six Day War, the Gaza Strip had existed under ambiguous circumstances, but substantively under Egyptian military occupation. After 1967, it followed other occupied territories under Israeli military administration until the Oslo Accords in 1993. Egypt renounced all claim to the territory in 1979, and after 1993, Gaza technically came under the jurisdiction of the Palestinian authority, even though the Israeli military still occupied it. Gaza remained, as it remains today, a substantively Palestinian enclave, and the center of radical opposition to Israel. Between 1967

---

[7] The Golan Heights were briefly re-held by Syria during the 1973 Yom Kippur War.
[8] In September 1971, in what came to be known as *Black September*, Jordan fought a de facto civil war against Palestinian factions in Jordan, supported by Syria and Lebanon. It was generally understood the Jordan's inferior status as an Arab nation offered the opportunity for Palestinians to take control of it, and declare it the Palestinian state that the region required as a basic element of peace.

and 2005, Israel established 21 Jewish settlements in Gaza, but all of them were uprooted following a complete withdrawal from the land. Shortly after, civil war erupted between the Palestinians, resulting in Hamas taking control of Gaza and using it as a base from which to conduct occasional attacks against Israel.

The question of Jewish settlements on the West Bank has probably been the most vexing issue created by the occupation. Israeli West Bank settlements began almost at the moment that the shooting stopped. The Israeli government formulated a plan to achieve this, the Allon Plan, which pictured a more general give and take of land and territory, but much of what occurred in regard to Israeli settlements did not closely follow this. Early settlements were military in character, and later expanded to include civilians. According to a secret document dating to 1970, obtained by *Haaretz*, an Israeli newspaper, the settlement of Kiryat Arba was established by confiscating land by military order and falsely representing the project as being strictly for military use, but in reality, Kiryat Arba was planned for settler use. The method of confiscating land by military order for establishing civilian settlements was an open secret in Israel throughout the 1970s, but the publication of the information was suppressed by the military censor.

By the 1970s and 1980s, Jewish settlements on the West Bank had become an open secret, and increasingly were falling under civil jurisdictions. The phenomenon played two obvious roles. First, it offered land and opportunity to Israeli Jews, and second, it established an increasing Jewish presence in what remains a disputed area. The West Bank is generally regarded as the only practical real estate available to create a substantive two-state solution between Israel and a future independent state of Palestine.

The Oslo Accords were a framework modeled after the goals of the Madrid Conference. The Accords provided for the establishment of the Palestinian Authority, which was headed by Yasser Arafat and Fatah. The Palestinian Authority would be given the responsibility for governing the Palestinians in the Gaza Strip and West Bank as the IDF gradually withdrew from parts of the territories and handed off security control to the PA. At the outset, the Israelis recognized the PLO as the Palestinian representative, clearing the way for the PLO's leadership to head the Palestinian Authority. Meanwhile, the PLO recognized Resolution 242, renounced terrorism, and recognized the right of Israel to exist in peace and security.

The Oslo Accords called for the IDF's withdrawal from parts of the territories in accordance with Resolution 242 over the course of a 5 year interim period, during which time the two sides were supposed to negotiate final status issues including East Jerusalem, Palestinian refugees, Jewish settlements, security, and final borders. These were deliberately left to be decided farther down the line, in order to give the parties room to generate progress and momentum during the initial steps that would make it more politically feasible for both sides to make tough choices.

On September 13, 1993, one of the iconic moments of the Middle East conflict took place in the Rose Garden, where Yasser Arafat shook hands with Yitzhak Rabin as President Clinton looked on. The signing of the Oslo Accords earned both men a Nobel Prize that year, like Begin and Sadat in 1978.

From the beginning, the Oslo Accords began suffering serious breakdowns. Israel's Likud party and other conservatives opposed the negotiations, which had barely passed Israel's Knesset. They also pointed to statements made by Arafat to Palestinian audiences in which he compared Oslo to a strategic truce signed by Muhammad with the tribe of Quraish that allowed Muhammad time to build up strength to vanquish his adversaries. Skeptical Israelis thus believed the Palestinians' goal was still to destroy Israel, and that the Palestinians simply viewed this as part of a gradual process that would make the end goal easier to accomplish. Meanwhile, Palestinians were skeptical that the Israelis would honor their side of the agreements, seeing resistance from conservatives and religious settlers in Israel as capable of derailing the Oslo Accords.

Moreover, the violence intensified after the Oslo Accords were signed. Most observers assumed that the violence was being carried out by extremists who hoped to stop the peace process, including Hamas and extreme Jewish settlers, but again both sides were skeptical that the other side was taking proper steps to guarantee security. The Palestinian Authority had renounced terrorism, but many in Israel now believed it was endorsing attacks, implying that Arafat and his group were complicit. At the same time, the "Cave of the Patriarchs" massacre in Hebron was carried out in February 1994 by extremist Jewish settler Baruch Goldstein, a follower of racist rabbi Meir Kahane and the Kach party, which had been banned in Israel in 1988.

Nevertheless, the two sides negotiated what came to be known as Oslo II, which were signed in Taba, Egypt on September 24, 1995. Oslo II established a detailed timeline that called for IDF forces to redeploy from certain areas of the Gaza Strip and Jericho in the West Bank, and eventually from major population centers in the West Bank, including Nablus, Kalkilya, Tulkarem, Ramallah, Bethlehem, Jenin and Hebron. Another phase called for the withdrawal of the IDF from about 450 smaller Palestinian settlements and villages in the West Bank.

Oslo II also established the idea of "safe passage," which would grant the Palestinians the ability to travel between the West Bank and Gaza, which were not connected by land.

On October 5, 1995, Prime Minister Rabin explained his rationale behind agreeing to Oslo II in a speech before the Knesset, outlining his vision of a permanent settlement with the Palestinians. Under Rabin's vision, Israelis would keep a military presence in the Jordan River Valley without annexing it, Israel would retain large settlement blocs near the Green Line, Jerusalem would remain undivided, and a Palestinian state would be demilitarized.

A month later, on November 4, 1995, Rabin was assassinated by a Jewish fanatic who sought to derail the Oslo Accords. Rabin's death was a huge blow to the Oslo Accords, even though his successor, Shimon Peres, attempted to continue moving the process forward. In May 1996, Peres lost the elections, as Likud leader Benjamin Netanyahu became Israel's new prime minister. An ardent opponent of the Oslo Accords, Netanyahu did agree to certain withdrawals after signing the Hebron Protocol and the Wye River Memorandum, but friction among his governing coalition made it impossible to continue withdrawals.

Although the Oslo Accords did not end up creating a lasting peace, they are still technically in effect. It is often said that everyone knows what the final peace agreement will look like, and there is indeed a consensus that there will be a limited right of return of Palestinian refugees, final borders that resemble the 1948 armistice lines with mutually agreed land swaps, and some sort of sharing of Jerusalem. However, neither side currently believes the other wants those, and political concerns also restrict the extent to which the sides can make concessions on issues like Jerusalem and the refugees.

Any peace deal between Israel and Syria will likely require the return of the Golan Heights, but this won't happen anytime soon as a result of the Syrian Civil War, as well as the involvement of Hezbollah and Iran, two of Israel's biggest antagonists today.

It also remains to be seen whether Hamas and the Palestinian Authority will actually work together or trust each other, or whether a unity government between the two that puts on a united front will suffer a "mask slipping" moment, as it did in 2007.

Meanwhile, over a million Arabs still live in Israel and even hold Knesset seats, while several million Palestinian Arabs live in the West Bank. It is often argued that the rising Palestinian population in the West Bank will eventually mean there's a Palestinian majority in Israel and the West Bank. President Obama made this claim in his May 2011 speech. The idea is that if the Palestinians in the West Bank outnumber the Jews in Israel and the West Bank settlements, Israel as an occupying force at that point will become an apartheid state and cease to be a democracy.

People continue to dispute whether the population rates and demographics will ever actually lead to a Palestinian majority in Israel and the West Bank, but it's a fear that caused radical philosophical changes in Likud leaders like Ariel Sharon. Many Israelis fear that the Palestinians continue to refuse offers in the hope of dropping demands for a two state solution and instead seek one binational state for both the Palestinians and Jews. With a Palestinian majority, Israel would cease to be a Jewish state.

Preamble to the Yom Kippur War

"Fight, Arabs. Let them know that we shall hang the last imperialist soldier with the entrails of the last Zionist." – Syrian government broadcast

The Bar Lev Line was a 93-mile-long series of fortifications stretching from the Mediterranean Coast to the Gulf of Suez, lying on the east bank of the Suez Canal. It comprised a network of trenches, tank traps, observation points, and bunkers, and its primary function was to act as a first line of defense against an Egyptian attack against the Israeli-held Sinai. Construction of the complex began soon after the Israeli occupation of the Sinai during the 1967 Six-Day War, and it was completed in the spring of 1970. On either side of this defensive divide, Israeli and Egyptian troops kept a careful eye on one another.

A picture of part of the line

Between the two armies lay the Suez Canal, 200 yards in width, flowing imperceptibly between the sand revetments that protected each side. The canal was closed, and as Israeli Defense Minister General Moshe Dayan was fond of remarking, it was nothing more than the world's best tank trap.

The Six-Day War had established Israel as a regional superpower, with a military capability out of all proportion to its size. At the same time, Israel's Arab neighbors were now united in one cause and one cause only, and that was the absolute annihilation of Israel. Israel may have toppled the giant in one bold and brilliant action and won the plaudits of military organizations worldwide, but it had made no friends. Victory, although absolute, did not put the matter to rest. Israel was surrounded on all sides by bitterly hostile enemies, and a follow-up war was inevitable. Israeli bulldozers and military engineers set to work immediately. The Golan Heights was heavily fortified, and along the length of the east bank of the Suez Canal, now in Israeli-occupied territory, work began on the Bar Lev Line.

No Arab leader felt the humiliation of the 1967 defeat more acutely than Egyptian President Nasser. He had great faith in his army's military prowess, so the fact it was brutally drubbed by an army so numerically inferior was a dishonor that simply could not be allowed to stand. Somehow, some way, Arab dignity must be restored. For the time being, however, Nasser was limited in what he could do. His army, in particular his air force and armored units, had been destroyed, and so all that remained was to close the Suez Canal to international shipping and pursue a low-level war of attrition against Israeli positions on the other side. This was a phase that came to be known in the international press as "No Peace, No War". A state of war still existed between the two sides, although no fighting on any particular scale was underway. Nonetheless, Nasser actively worked to rebuild his army, utilizing his strategic alliance with the Soviet Union. "What was taken by force," he was often heard to say, "can only be restored by force."

The stalemate, however, was broken in 1970, when Nasser, a larger-than-life figure, died of a heart attack. Power devolved to his deputy and long-time associate, Anwar Sadat. Sadat brought to the office of Egyptian president none of the charisma of his predecessor, and it was generally assumed that his exercise of power would last only so long as the next coup.

Sadat

Sadat, however, surprised his detractors. He was an ex-military officer and a seasoned political brawler, and he proved to have more in him than most expected. He was certainly more cautious, more pragmatic, and perhaps more astute. He was also, uniquely among Arab leaders, prepared to acknowledge the fact that Israel, for better or worse, was a fixture on the Middle Eastern map, and that the practical possibility of removing it had been lost in previous wars. The question now was simply a restoration of Arab pride, and although he was no less committed to a third war than Nasser, he was perhaps more reasonable in his objectives. A return to pre-1967 positions, therefore, became the basis of his strategic planning, after which he began to look around at a changed global dynamic with a view to establishing the army necessary to achieve this.

By the time Sadat took over from Nasser in late September 1970, a great deal had changed. Stalin and Khrushchev were dead, and Leonid Brezhnev was in power in the Kremlin. Richard Nixon was in the White House, the Cold War was in effect, and the nuclear arms race had begun. Both superpowers, while covertly spreading their influence worldwide, were assiduously avoiding direct confrontation with one another.

Nasser, from an aggressively anti-imperial platform, had positioned Egypt firmly within the Soviet camp. Sadat, on the other hand, although retaining old alliances, began to appreciate the greater value of an eventual Egyptian alliance with the West. This became part of his long-term thinking, and as he began to map out a war strategy, he did so in Clausewitzian terms, envisaging war as an instrument of politics and not, as Nasser had tended to do, as an aim and objective unto itself. Sadat pictured a limited war in pursuit of three key objectives: to satisfy national pride, to shift the current political logjam, and to present the United States with an opportunity to engage with Egypt. In exchange for an Egyptian shift from the Soviet to the U.S. sphere of influence, Egypt would require that appropriate pressure to be brought to bear by the U.S., the only nation with such leverage, on Israel to withdraw from the Sinai Peninsula.

Sadat also held the Suez Canal, which had been closed since 1967. In exchange for even a partial Israeli withdrawal from the Canal Zone, Sadat offered to clear obstructions and re-open the canal to international shipping, including Israeli ships. This, however, served only to stir up animosity and suspicion on the part of Sadat's fellow Arab leaders, who saw it as a disgraceful retreat from war and a dangerous experiment in engagement with Israel.

Despite his critics, war did indeed remain key to Sadat's strategy; it would just be a different kind of war. The mood of his nation demanded war, the Egyptians wanted payback, and somehow Sadat had to give it to them. Speaking to a domestic audience, he declared 1971 to be the "Year of Decision", promising that in the near future, a "Battle of Destiny" between Egypt and Israel would be fought. This was fighting talk, to be sure, but as 1971 slipped away and no such battle took place, the Israelis stood down and began to regard Sadat's aggressive posturing as just a poorer version of Nasser's. The Israeli victories of 1948 and 1967 had established the belief in Israel that the IDF was invincible. A combination of air and armor, supported by excellent intelligence, remained the basis of Israeli defense strategy, and so long as Egypt lacked a comparable air strike and defense capability, there was no threat.

Egypt, of course, was not Israel's only belligerent neighbor. Both Jordan and Syria had lost territory to Israel in 1967, and both represented a potential threat. Jordan, however, had slipped somewhat lower on that scale in recent years, thanks to an uneasy accommodation with Israel, a pragmatic move on the part of King Hussein that secured him very few friends among his fellow Arab leaders.

Syria, on the other hand, remained entirely unreconciled and was deeply rancorous and troubled by the continued Israeli occupation of the Golan Heights. With the assumption of power in Syria in March 1971 of Hafez al-Assad, a pro-Soviet ex-Air Force officer, a potential second front opened up on Israel's northern border. Unlike the uneasy ceasefire in effect along the Suez

Canal, the Israeli Northern Front, comprising the Golan Heights, was regularly rocked by aircraft and artillery duels between Syrian and Israeli forces.

Hafez al-Assad

King Hussein of Jordan

Despite these threats, Israel was far more concerned with the high-profile activities of militant Palestinian groups like the PLO. A de facto war was fought in 1970 between the Jordanian government and various PLO factions, and Israeli athletes were murdered by PLO terrorists at the 1972 summer Olympics in Munich.

The Israeli Illusion

"Our American friends offer us money, arms, and advice. We take the money, we take the arms, and we decline the advice." – Moshe Dayan

For all of its contradictions and turbulence, no one anticipated imminent war in the Middle East. The Arab world was seen as divided, mutually antagonistic, and full with internal discords, incapable of coordinated action. Israel, on the other hand, presented a united front, powerful and unbreakable. Backed by the United States and with an unimpeachable military record, nobody in the world would predict Arab success in a conventional war.

On the eve of the Six-Day War, Israeli General Moshe Dayan was appointed Israeli Defense Minister. Dayan was an iconic member of the Israeli defense establishment, with a patch worn over his right eye and the air of a battle-scarred warrior about him. It was he who determined that the opportunity presented by the Six-Day War should be seized to gain as much buffer territory from Israel's neighbors as possible, while at the same time smashing the Arab armies to a degree that would set them back for decades.

Dayan and President Nixon in 1970

After the war and the achievement of these objectives, he set about establishing the future manual of Israeli warfare. The lesson that was learned as a consequence of the Six-Day War was simply that, within the specifics of the Middle Eastern theater, a combination of tanks, aircraft, and intelligence would always prevail. Of these three pillars of Israeli defense, air power stood supreme. Air power had won the Six-Day War, and it stood to reason that until the Arab coalition could function in unity, and until the various states achieved parity with Israel in air power, no true threat existed.

Intelligence was the second key element of the Israeli strategy.[9] On the eve of the Six-Day War, thanks largely to the superb performance of the various Israeli intelligence agencies, Israeli military planners were able to utilize detailed and intimate intelligence concerning Arab planning, force levels, capabilities, deployments, and dispositions. A combination of well-placed human and technological assets, aided by deplorable Arab security, gave the Israeli military establishment all the forewarning necessary to plan the pre-emptive campaign. Such effective intelligence gathering and analysis, indeed, offered the two other pillars of Israeli defense (air and armor) the freedom of movement over the battlefield to affect a victory of almost surreal proportions.

By 1973, the Israeli Director of Military Intelligence, Major General Eliyahu Zeira, felt sufficient confidence in the capability of his agency that he predicted at least 48 hours forewarning of any major Arab movement against Israel. This would allow for ample time to mobilize reserves and gain mastery of the air. As a consequence of this, all plans established by the IDF to meet such a contingency were based on this projection.

---

[9] Israeli intelligence has traditionally been divided into four main branches. The oldest and best known is the Mossad. The Mossad is configured as an external espionage agency responsible for intelligence collection, covert operations, and counterterrorism. The Shin Bet covers internal intelligence and security agency, while AMAN, the Directorate of Military Intelligence, is concerned primarily with military intelligence and the analysis and evaluation of internationally gathered intelligence.

Zeira

Israel, of course, could never match its neighbors in manpower, so air power became the main equalizer. By 1973, over half of the Israeli defense budget was allocated to the IAF, and by the end of 1972, the Israelis could field some 500 combat aircraft, including American A-4G Skyhawk and F4 Phantoms and French Mirage and Mystere fighter jets. This formidable arsenal was poised against an Egyptian air fleet comprising some 550 primarily Soviet MiG 17s, 19s, and 21s, along with a handful of Sukhoi SU-7s. In combination with the Syrian Air Force, similarly supplied, the Israelis were significantly outnumbered, but with a substantial superiority in technology and training, particularly in missile technology, there would seem to be every justification for the confidence felt by the IAF and the Israeli central command.

In armor deployment, the Israelis also relied on superior tactics and training to make the best of what they had. By the 1970s, it was firmly established in IDF doctrine that the quick and aggressive use of air and armor assets would always be the most effective formula to deal with the understood strategy of any future Arab aggression. As a result, in the aftermath of 1967, the Israelis were somewhat guilty of preparing to fight the last war. This did not go unobserved; as Sadat pored over his maps, chain-smoking cigarettes and planning his next decisive move, he wondered how best to exploit this Israeli complacency.

At the same time, Sadat went about cutting back the powers of the much-hated secret police and set about dismantling the police state created by Nasser and his pro-Soviet advisors.[10] The

Corrective Revolution was indeed a great success in terms of the immense approval he received from his people, an also in terms of setting himself apart from the harsh and closed-off rule of Nasser. It demonstrated Sadat's intuitive grasp of what his people truly wanted, and his willingness to give them exactly that; political prisons were permanently shut down, tapes and transcripts of private telephone conversations held by the Interior Ministry were destroyed, and the arbitrary arrests that had become so rampant during Nasser 's rule were halted.

Sadat continued to have difficult relations with the Soviet Union. Ever since the Suez crisis and the Soviet Union's clear refusal to come to Egypt's aid, Sadat had been greatly suspicious of the superpower and its intentions. Since Sadat took the presidency, various negotiations were held with the Soviets, and several treaties were signed, but these were mostly to mollify the Soviet Union and keep its leaders from discerning Sadat's true stance toward his fickle ally. Relations between the two countries continued to deteriorate. Weapons deals were made, but the weapons never arrived. Soviet politburo members promised him arms, but they never came. Sadat traveled to Moscow numerous times to inquire about these promised weapons, but he was always brushed off and returned home empty-handed.

In July 1972, Sadat surprised his nation, the region, and the world when he abruptly ordered all 15,000 Soviet advisors and military experts stationed in Egypt to leave the country within a week. Sadat also demanded all Soviet equipment to be sold to Egypt, or to also be taken out of Egypt within a week. An angry Moscow responded by recalling all of its citizens and equipment, flying them back to the Soviet Union in haste.[11] The move was so unexpected that it surprised even the United States, as Sadat had asked for nothing from the U.S. in exchange for expelling the Soviet advisors.

As impulsive as Sadat's exasperated decision to teach the Soviets a lesson may have been, it was also deemed necessary from a long-term perspective. It was becoming clear to Sadat that the Soviet Union was using arms supplies and deals as a means of controlling Egyptian foreign policy, and Moscow's arrogant and condescending attitude toward Cairo did nothing to ameliorate the situation, instead exacerbating it to such a degree that Sadat was forced to take action. The move was immensely popular with his people; yet again, he was correcting past wrongs and truly taking into account the will of the Egyptian people.

A New Strategy

"Russians can give you arms but only the United States can give you a solution." – Anwar Sadat

Sadat settled early on the limited objective of returning Egypt to its pre-1967 status. This simply meant a return of the Sinai Peninsula and Gaza. Destroying Israel was no longer feasible, and he wasted no time planning it. If an Israeli withdrawal from the West Bank and the Golan Heights could be negotiated, then all would be well and good.

When Sadat's conservative military establishment were briefed on this, they resisted, insisting on total war. In October 1972, therefore, at a meeting of the Supreme Council of the Armed Forces, he purged his War Minister, General Muhammad Sadiq; his deputy; and various other key commanders. Sadiq was replaced by the 55-year-old General Ahmad Ismail Ali, a less innovative defense official, but compliant and loyal. Appointed Chief-of-Staff was 50-year-old Lieutenant General Saad Mohamed el-Husseiny el-Shazly, previously commander of Egyptian

---

[10] Eric Pace, "Anwar El-Sadat, the Daring Arab Pioneer of Peace with Israel," *The New York Times*, October 7, 1981, http://www.nytimes.com/learning/general/onthisday/bday/1225.html.
[11] Carroll, *Anwar Sadat*, 65

special forces, and confirmed as director of operations was 51-year-old Lieutenant General Mohammed Abed El-Ghani El-Gamasi, a former tank commander, but perhaps better known as a director of intelligence. At the senior command level, Air Vice Marshal Hosni Mubarak was appointed commander of the air force. In 1981, as deputy president, Mubarak would assume power upon Sadat's assassination, emerging afterward as one of the most influential and controversial Egyptian presidents of recent times. Numerous other new appointments were made, and by the end of 1972, Sadat had created a senior command comprising a corps of strategic, forward thinking, but most importantly, loyal military commanders.

Mubarak and President George W. Bush

This change very quickly filtered down the ranks. Sadat's predecessor, Nasser, had allowed his own rise to power through the mechanics of a coup to influence his attitude to the junior command of his army. He avoided as much as possible an educated officer corps, which tended to diminish the leadership quality and professionalism of the army from a brigade level downward. The new senior command introduced a far higher proportion of urban recruits and university-educated junior officers, which had the effect of improving not only the mechanized and armored sections, but also the quality of general tactical command.

Sadat knew he had numbers on his side, and with this in mind, he began to conceive a bold strategy of launching a massive, divisional assault along the entire length of the Suez Canal. This would immediately overwhelm the Bar Lev Line and would disperse pressure in a manner that would confuse the Israelis in the first few vital hours over the exact location of the Egyptian main effort. As the Israelis rushed to mobilize their response, Egyptian bridgeheads could be established and the heavy armored divisions brought across to the east bank. An eastward advance of just a few miles would then be made before Egyptian forces would dig in and await the inevitable Israeli counterattack.

Depending on the outcome of this, Egyptian forces would either move to seize the strategically important Mitla and Gidi Passes, essential to the mobilization of Israeli reserves, or simply remain in occupation of a limited strip of the Sinai. [12] The latter option would be simpler, requiring no great strategic maneuver other than to hold firm against Israeli-armored assaults long enough to wait for a UN ceasefire and appeal for intervention by the Cold War superpowers. If Syria could be brought on board, then, ideally, at that point, Syria would be in possession of the Golan Heights, and it too could enter negotiations under UN and superpower supervision based on current positions. It would be difficult to argue against a fait accompli, and upon that, the Arabs could claim victory.

Key to the success of this plan was to deal quickly with the inevitable and rapid onrush of Israeli air and tank defenses, and for this Sadat looked east. Anti-tank and anti-aircraft missile systems had advanced significantly in the years since 1967 and would be an addition to the modern battlefield that the Israelis had not yet factored into their standard battlefield manual. Nor were Israeli tanks equipped with night vision equipment, which modern Soviet tanks were. Moreover, the Soviets, developing these weapons systems, were anxious to see them tested in the field, although perhaps not in the context of an actual war. The Arab propensity for spectacular defeat might not bode well for the reputation of Soviet arms.

However, Sadat pictured a heavy saturation of anti-aircraft missile placements along the west bank of the canal in order to limit the ability of the IAF to strike into Egyptian airspace and offering advance infantry and tank units air cover up to 20 miles east of the Suez line. A further saturation of forward infantry advance units with sophisticated anti-tank weaponry, also within the Soviet inventory, would provide the vital David and Goliath factor.

Thus, in February 1973, even after he had taken steps to counter Soviet influence in Egypt, Sadat visited Moscow, and his shopping list was extensive. Besides the necessary SAM-2, SAM-3, and SAM-6 anti-aircraft missile systems, he requested batteries of state-of-the-art SCUD missiles with sufficient range to threaten Israeli cities. To deal with tanks, he was given a supply of Soviet AT-3 *Sagger* portable anti-tank missiles systems. These were infantry portable units, wire guided and operated using a joystick, and although considerable training was required to use them, they would prove to be the vital force multiplier.

Meanwhile, a high-level series of meetings began between Egypt and Syria, resulting in an agreement in principal that the campaign would be conducted substantively on two fronts. Syrian president Assad, passionately anti-Israel, was initially in disagreement over the idea of a limited strategic objective. In the end, however, he too was brought around to the reality that Israel was there to stay, but he retained the option of doing much more than simply reclaiming the Golan Heights if the opportunity presented itself.

An important point in these discussions, which would impact later events, was an understanding that Assad either assumed from discussions or was explicitly led to believe that the Egyptian advance would be in two phases. The first phase would involve crossing the Suez Canal and establishing bridgeheads, and the second would be a rapid movement inland to seize the two most important Sinai Passes: the Gidi and Mitla. Around this, Assad planned a lightning, conventional armored advance on the Golan Heights to correspond with the initial Egyptian crossing of the Suez Canal and upon the assumption that the Egyptian army would then begin a land offensive over a wide front, absorbing all available Israeli armor and manpower. The Syrians would then exploit the overextended IDF to commence a movement south down the Jordan Valley and into Israeli-populated territory.

What remained then was simply to agree on a Zero Hour, or Y-Day, the precise day and hour that the operation would commence.[13] This was dictated somewhat by the tidal conditions that

---

[12] The Mitla and Gidi Passes are two main access routes through the rugged interior of the Sinai Peninsula, which at the time would be vital for the movement of Israeli armor and infantry reinforcements to the front line.

affected the Suez Canal, and the necessity of using various types of pontoon bridges at a number of predetermined points. An initial date in May 1973 was chosen, a time when hydrographic and lunar conditions would both be optimum, but this was pushed back by the fact that the Syrians were now on board, making it necessary to further integrate planning and strategy.[14]

In the end, the date chosen was October 6, and this was for a variety of reasons. First, tidal and lunar conditions were once again optimal, but also the day happened to fall on both the Jewish holiday of Yom Kippur and the Muslim festival of Ramadan. On that day, holy for both sides, the capacity for Israeli reserves to be mobilized would be at its lowest, while at the same time, the Israelis would hardly expect the Arabs to mount a major operation on their most sacred season of the year. Since October 6 was the Tenth Day of Ramadan, the traditional anniversary of the Battle of Badr, won by the prophet Muhammad in the year 626, the pending war acquired the codename Operation *Badr*.

The Syrian strategy, without the complication of the Suez Canal, was reasonably simple. The topography of the Golan Heights allowed for the advance of a substantial invasion force, spearheaded by armor and supported by artillery, mechanized infantry, and anti-aircraft defense. Israeli positions would be overwhelmed, and the Syrian army would simply reoccupy the Golan Heights.

Sadat, on the other hand, had a far more complicated nut to crack. The Suez Canal separates Africa from the Levant, and it is about 100 miles in length and over 200 yards wide on average. The main logistical obstacle, however, was not the water, but the sand embankment rising some 30 feet on what was then the Israeli side. It comprised debris from the original construction of the canal, added to by years of dredging and modified into a static defense by the Israelis. It was a formidable obstacle. n a worse-case scenario, the Egyptians would need to plan on a muscular Israeli armored response within 15 minutes, perhaps a little longer, but certainly within an hour, so the initial crossing and a breach of the sand wall had to be achieved in that time.

Various strategies were devised and tested on a side branch of the canal, along with a great deal of head scratching and experimentation. In the end, however, a simple and ingenious solution was arrived at. During the construction of the Aswan Dam in the early 1960s, a system of moving quantities of sand was deployed using high pressure water jets. This was tried on sand revetments, and it was found to work perfectly. Thereafter, the necessary pumps were procured, mounted on floating platforms, and some eight detachments were formed and relentlessly drilled to undertake this all-important breaching operation.

Meanwhile, much of the success of the pending operation would depend on absolute secrecy, and initially, the signs were good. All indications were that the Israelis had no idea at all that a major assault was afoot. In the spring of 1973, just months before the operation and as advanced preparations were well underway, Israeli Director General of Military Intelligence, General Eli Zei'ra, casually observed in an interview with a *London Times* reporter: "I discount the likelihood of a conventional Arab attack. The biggest problem Israeli intelligence faces is to underestimate what we're up against, but an equally big risk is that we would overestimate (and thus over-react). They (Arab leadership) have their own logic. Thus we have to look hard for evidence of their real intentions in the field, otherwise, with the Arabs, all you have is rhetoric. Too many Arab leaders have intentions which far exceed their capabilities."

This sentiment was shared in general across Israel, where it was assumed the Arabs would

---

[13] Y-Day was so named because the word 'Yom' means 'Day' in both Hebrew and Arabic.

[14] Initially, it was understood that Jordan would not take part in the major operation, but that Jordanian armed forces would demonstrate along the east bank of the Jordan River in order to preoccupy as many IDF assets in defense of a potential third front as possible.

never mount a comprehensive operation against Israel before achieving air parity. The Israelis worked off a simple blueprint that they referred to as the "Concept", and this decreed that the defensive capability of the Bar Lev Line would hold back any attempt to cross the Suez Canal long enough for the mobilization of an Israeli air and armored response. It was also inconceivable to a majority of Israelis, within or without the defense establishment, that an Arab attack would not be detected by Israeli intelligence at least 48 hours before its launch. Moreover, should any of Israel's enemies have the audacity to launch such an attack, defeat would be inevitable and as rapid and comprehensive as it was 1967.

Much of this confidence was justified, and certainly, if Egyptian and Syrian planning had conformed to tradition, then all would have been well. However, historians of the Yom Kippur War, while differing widely in their interpretation of many of the details, all tend to agree that a catastrophic Israeli intelligence failure was most to blame for the events that would play out over the next few weeks. For example, the major Syrian force build-up went on behind the lines, but these were difficult to hide. From observation points on Mount Hermon and the uplands of the Golan, Syrian activity was open to view. However, a serendipitous event occurred in the weeks prior to the operation that offered a plausible reason for why the Syrians would be massing on their side of the ceasefire line. On September 13, a routine Israeli air reconnaissance overflight of Syria provoked a major dogfight. When it was all over, 12 Syrian MiGs had been shot down with the loss of one Israeli Mirage. In the light of this, some sort of a Syrian demonstration could certainly be expected, and thus, accelerated military activity along the ceasefire line was not altogether unexpected.

For their part, the Egyptians began their advance preparations behind announced military maneuvers, which were not an infrequent occurrence and which did not, in and of themselves, alert Israeli forward observation positions to anything untoward. Several weeks in advance of the operation, Sadat's national security advisor, Hafez Ismail, embarked on a tour of Western capitals preaching peace and rapprochement in the region. As he did, Sadat's Foreign Minister, Mohammed Zayyat, pursued a similar diplomatic mission in the East, creating in combination the impression that Sadat was committed to some sort of peaceful resolution of the Middle East situation.

Sadat, meanwhile, had attended a September conference of the Non-Aligned Movement in Algeria, a month before the launch of the operation, where he appeared exhausted and ill and thus stayed out of public view. In the meantime, Egyptian intelligence services undertook a high-profile search for a suitable location in Europe from where the Egyptian president could seek medical treatment. None of this tended to support any theories that the Arabs were about to go to war, and the Israelis seemed on the whole to be satisfied that this was true.

Then, on September 28, a fortnight before Y-Day, two gunmen of *As-Sa'iqa*, a Syrian-based Palestinian guerrilla organization allied to the PLO, seized a train in Austria, taking hostages and demanding the closure of Schonau Castle near Vienna, which at that time was being used as a transit facility for Jews exiting the Soviet Union en-route to Israel. The Austrian Chancellor, Bruno Kreisky, himself a non-observant Jew, agreed to the demand, provoking outrage in Israel.

This had the dual effect of diverting Israeli attention, but also providing further possible reasons why the Arabs may wish to bolster their security presence on their borders with Israel. The Israelis might well be expected to launch reprisal raids, in the expectation of which Israel's Arab neighbors had every right to be prepared.

Amassed on the west bank of the Suez Canal, however, under reasonably clear Israeli scrutiny, a formidable Egyptian force was quietly taking up its positions. The total strength of the

Egyptian Army at the time was some 800,000 troops, 2,000 tanks, 2,300 artillery pieces, 150 anti-aircraft batteries, and 550 first-line aircraft. These forces were divided into two field armies: the Second Army and the Third Army. The Second Army occupied the northern sector — broadly speaking from the northern extremity of the Suez Canal at its junction with the Mediterranean to the north bank of the Great Bitter Lake — while the Third Army occupied the southern sector, from the north bank of the Great Bitter lake to the port of Suez at the head of the Red Sea. The First Army would remain in reserve on the west bank.

On the northern front, the Syrian buildup was no less formidable. At any given time, about 110,000 men served in the Syrian armed forces, out of which perhaps 100,000 were in the army. This number could be doubled in an emergency through the mobilization of reserves. The combat element of the army consisted of two armored and three mechanized infantry divisions, seven artillery regiments, and a paratroop and special forces brigade. By 1973, the Syrian army had been modernized significantly by the supply of Soviet equipment, replacing much that had been lost in 1967. By the end of 1972, Syria could field, more or less, 800 tanks and self-propelled guns, 500 other light armored vehicles, 800 various artillery pieces, and eight batteries of SAM anti-aircraft missiles.

The Enemy

"Israel wants to make it clear to the government of Egypt that it has no aggressive intentions whatsoever against any Arab state at all." – Israeli Prime Minister Levi Eshkol

The Bar Lev Line was defended by 450 Israeli troops and 91 tanks, spread across 35 widely spaced fortifications. The Bar Lev Line was, from its original conception, a controversial idea that did not conform to the original strategy when the IDF took control of the Sinai Peninsula. The idea behind doing so was simply to provide strategic depth in an environment that was ideal for mobile, armored maneuver. The placement of any static defense system tended to cut across conventional Israeli thinking, insofar as a successful breach of the Bar Lev Line would immediately isolate a large force of Israeli soldiers behind enemy lines. In October 1973, this is precisely what would occur.

Notwithstanding the Bar Lev Line and the deployments associated with it, the general Israeli defense strategy was codenamed *Shovach Yonim*, or *Dovecote*, and it was founded almost entirely on the 300 tanks of the Israeli Sinai Division, the only armored division of the standing army, backed up by the Israeli Air Force. The obvious defensive positions in the Sinai were the passes and the offensive zone, the open desert between the mountainous mass of central Sinai and the Suez, which suited a war of armored maneuver and which, of course, quite naturally favored the Israelis. However, very little, if any thought appeared to have been given to fighting a defensive battle. The emphasis remained on a swift counterattack that would carry Israeli forces, air and armor, quickly across the canal and into Egyptian territory. This was the essential element of *Dovecote*. An additional operational plan, codenamed *Sela*, or *Rock*, required simply the prompt mobilization of reserves, primarily armored reserves, which accounted for the bulk of Israeli Defense Force fighting capability, based on the assumption of a minimum forewarning of 48 hours.

As a result, the entire Israeli defense strategy in the Sinai rested on the rapid containment of any aggressive advance by the 300 tanks of the Sinai Division, permanently in position in the Sinai, which would either spearhead a counterattack or hold an invasion. Beyond that, no plan existed.

Around the end of September 1973, a trickle of information began to reach the ears of Israeli intelligence of large-scale mobilizations taking place on the Egyptian side. Nightly reports were returned to the military command bunker in Tel Aviv of convoys under the escort of military police moving in the direction of the canal. AMAN, however, aware of the commencement of Egyptian autumn maneuvers, attributed all Egyptian military movement to this and continued to advise a low probability of war. Likewise, a corresponding Syrian build-up was attributed to the September air incident and anxieties following the Schonau Castle episode.

All of this might, under the circumstances, have been understandable, but on the evening of September 25, King Hussein of Jordan made a covert helicopter flight to Israel to warn the Israeli authorities that war was imminent. His dates and times were uncertain, but the fact that an Arab national leader, in a difficult diplomatic position, had made the effort to warn Israel should have given the warning plenty of credibility.

The intelligence issue certainly appears to have been the signature Israeli failure as the countdown to war began. Given that, various reports, books, histories, and analyses written about events leading up to the war tend to blame almost without exception Israel's military intelligence chief, General Eli Zeira. Forward observation units in the Sinai and on the Golan Heights were certainly reporting that something was afoot, and increasingly urgent intelligence briefs were finding their way onto Zeira's desk, which he either ignored or interpreted according to the "Concept."

It was not until the families of Soviet and allied advisors in Egypt and Syria were evacuated that the truth began to dawn. Israeli intelligence analysts were initially puzzled by this development, and for the first time, a note of alarm began to creep into official discussion. Much else so far had been easily explainable, but this was not. Then, the director of the Mossad, Zvi Zamir, received an urgent summons to London from what was described as an impeccable source. In more recent accounts of the war, this source has been tentatively identified as Ashraf Marwan, a son-in-law of Nasser and Sadat's serving information secretary. On the same day, Friday, October 5, a day before the Yom Kippur holiday, a meeting of senior IDF officers was convened that included both Dayan and Zeira, as well as Lieutenant General David Elazar, Chief of Staff, and his deputy, Major General Israel Tal. The group met to discuss unfolding developments, and with the most recent aerial surveillance spread out before them, a sober sense of the pending situation at last began to dawn. It was still not absolutely certain that war was imminent, and in view of Yom Kippur, there was a reluctance among the operational chiefs to issue orders for a general mobilization. Instead, a "C" Alert, the highest alert short of war, was ordered. All leaves were cancelled and the emergency mobilization network was placed on standby. Additional armored reinforcement was ordered to the Golan, and a brigade was dispatched to the Sinai on the understanding that, even against significant odds, current force deployments on both fronts were, for the time being, adequate.

Zamir, in the meantime, arrived in London and met with his source, who informed him that a two-pronged Arab attack was planned for the following day. Zamir was sufficiently impressed by this to get on the telephone immediately, and bearing in mind time differences, the news was received in Tel Aviv in the early hours of the morning on October 6. The first to receive it was Zamir's chief of bureau, who obtained it in code, after which it was passed on to a handful of key men and one woman, Israeli Prime Minister Golda Meir.

Golda Meir

Zero Hour had not as yet been specified, but by 6:00 that morning, a meeting of the General Staff was underway. General Elezar's first telephone call upon hearing the news was to the head of the Israeli Air Force, Lieutenant General Benyamin Peled, confirming whether the IAF was prepared for an immediate pre-emptive strike against Syrian SAM batteries. This was confirmed, and authorization for a strike was given pending ministerial approval. Ministerial approval, however, was denied. The intelligence was compelling, but it remained unconfirmed. A preemptive strike would simply position Israel as the aggressor, which would undermine the possibility of a later appeal to the United States for assistance. Prime Minister Meir assured Israel's Arab neighbors through the international diplomatic network that they need fear no Israeli attack, but that an Arab attack against Israel would be dealt with swiftly and effectively.

On the other side of the world, U.S. Secretary of State Henry Kissinger was awakened with the news that war in the Middle East was imminent. Israel's public posture was, of course, bold and determined, but private communications between Kissinger and the office of the Israeli Prime Minister confirmed that the Israelis might be in trouble. Kissinger immediately contacted the Soviet Ambassador to Washington, Anatoly Dobrynin, to whom he repeated Israel's assurances that no Israeli offensive was planned. He then contacted the Israeli *chargé d'affaires* in Washington and briefed him on his conversation with Donrynin, earnestly appealing to the Israelis to do nothing rash.

Kissinger and President Gerald Ford

As this was happening, Zamir's intelligence report was strengthened by Israeli Foreign Minister Abba Eban, who happened then to be in New York attending the 28th session of the UN General Assembly and had somehow ascertained that hostilities would break out at 6:00 that night. That was actually four hours later than the agreed Arab Y-Hour.

Along the Suez Canal, Israeli troops scrambled to dig in, while the Egyptians divisions, poised just a few hundred yards away, made final checks and preparations. A few minutes before 2:00 p.m., Egyptian President Anwar Sadat entered Centre Ten, the Egyptian command center located in Cairo, and there he took his seat for the commencement of Operation *Badr*.

The Start of the Yom Kippur War

"We didn't have any reserves left, there was nothing left. The war was perceived not just at a critical, almost hopeless stage, but as a struggle for our very physical survival." – General Israel Tal

At almost precisely 2:00 p.m. on October 6, 1973, a wave of assault aircraft screamed over the Suez Canal and into Israeli occupied territory, releasing a payload of bombs and other ordnance on a series of selected targets. Israeli command centers, air bases, anti-aircraft missile batteries, and radar stations across the Sinai were hit, and as the first wave of aircraft returned to their bases to rearm and refuel, an artillery barrage of 2,000 guns opened up along the entire length of the militarized zone, delivering upwards of 10,000 shells on Israeli positions in just over a minute. Egyptian tanks and flat trajectory guns were hoisted atop a series of pre-prepared revetments, from where they were able to rain down fire across the canal into exposed Israeli positions.

A picture of Egyptian aircraft over the Bar Lev Line on October 6

Under cover of this firestorm, a force of some 4,000 mixed infantry and commandos took to the water in a flotilla of inflatable dinghies and wooden boats, beginning a rapid traverse of the Suez Canal. Once on the east bank, the leaders scrambled up the steep sides of the 30-foot sand wall, from where they rolled down and secured rope ladders. Laden with an assortment of weapons, most crucially an array of Soviet-supplied anti-tank systems, Egyptian infantry followed, racing forward and often bypassing the Israeli fortifications wherein stunned Israeli reservists and conscripts were taking cover and watching. The attackers continued on to an average depth of just over a mile into the desert, and there they dug in to await the inevitable Israeli armored response.

Behind them, water cannons began breaching the sand wall as pontoon bridges were laid, and within a few hours, the first tanks and armored vehicles were moving across the canal. Further south, in what is known as the Bitter Lakes, brackish stretches of open water a little over midway down the canal, amphibious vehicles were moving across, carrying commando and infantry units. By early evening, two divisional bridgeheads had been established, some 3 miles long and a little over a mile deep, behind which armor and equipment continued to move across. The bridgeheads widened steadily, and as the first dust plume on the horizon indicated the arrival of Israeli tanks, the Egyptians were prepared.

A picture of amphibious vehicles crossing the canal

The first Israeli tanks to appear on the scene paused for a moment to take stock of the situation, and seeing nothing other than their traditional foes, they began to advance. As they came within a mile or so of Egyptian positions, however, infantrymen stepped out of foxholes and assembled their laborious missile launchers, sending missiles across the no-man's land in a lacework of white vapor trails and into the lead tanks. Overhead, Israeli Air Force jets blundered into the Egyptian air shield, targeting Egyptian pontoon bridges, but they soon began to register a wall of incoming anti-aircraft fire and were pushed back with casualties.

A picture of wreckage from an Israeli plane in the Sinai

It became immediately clear to the Israeli command in the sector, headed by General Shmuel Gonen, that the defenders of the Bar Lev Line were now defending nothing but their own positions and lives.[15] Within a few hours, plotting on a map the flood of reports coming into his bunker, it became clear to Gonen that a major amphibious operation was underway along the entire length of the canal, but without any immediately identifiable "main effort." Gonen was a soldier schooled in the Dovecote doctrine, and for the required armored assault to be ordered, and bearing in mind the requirement for an Israeli attack across the canal, he needed to determine a specific point to direct his armor.

The three brigades of the Sinai Division were commanded by Major-General Albert Mandler, under whom served three colonels: Gaby Amir to the north, Amnon Reshef at the center, and Dan Shomron further south. Mandler's preliminary order was for a cautious advance on the canal, but without initial reconnaissance, and as the afternoon sun set in their eyes, the tank commanders had no idea what to expect. What they encountered, however, were well dug-in, well-trained, and coordinated Egyptian advance positions from where the first shock of anti-tank ordnance hit, knocking out the lead tanks. Egyptian infantrymen were, of course, vulnerable to artillery fire, but at that point the Israelis had only about 50 artillery pieces along a 100-mile front, and these were already under heavy counter-battery fire.

The picture that was returned to the Gonen, however, and then to Elazar in Tel Aviv, reflected a more ordered advance than was actually taking place. The desperate plight of the Bar Lev defenders was not fully appreciated, so no immediate order was given for their relief. What the fog of war hid was a bold series of tank advances suffering heavy losses at the hands of Egyptian anti-tank teams and the devolution of the Bar Lev Line into pockets of isolated troops fighting off determined Egyptian infantry assaults. The *Dovecote* strategy was crumbling against the unexpected ferocity and coordination of Egyptian attacking forces.

---

[15] The main military installation in the Sinai was situated some 50 km from the canal, at Bir Gifgafa, known by the Israelis as Redafin, where a large military complex contained the HQ of southern command.

A picture of wrecked Israeli Patton tanks in the Sinai

If the situation along the Suez Canal was obscure, the situation along the Golan Heights was even more so. The Golan comprises a series of low hills and valleys in the shadow of Mount Hermon to the north and the rugged Yarmuk Valley to the south, which marks the border with Jordan. To the west is the Sea of Galilee, and to the east is the Syrian capital of Damascus. Roughly from north to south run two roads: the Ceasefire Road and the TAP road, or Tapline Road, following the underground Trans-Arabian Pipeline (TAP) that originates in Saudi Arabia and crosses the Golan en route to Lebanon. Five lateral roads cross from west to east, leading into Israel, with bridges spanning the River Jordan.

Confronting the Israelis along the Purple Line, or the ceasefire line, was a conventional force of three Syrian divisions, with a strong armored brigade of some 200 tanks per division. Two further armored divisions were deployed to the rear, with the addition of a handful of independent brigades. This brought the total of Syrian tanks poised to assault the heights to approximately 1,500, supported by perhaps 1,000 artillery pieces deployed in 600 units. The Syrian tanks were mostly Soviet T-62 pattern, supported by a mechanized infantry of about 150,000 men, further supported by tanks, and including 800 or more armored troop carriers.

Defending the Heights was an Israeli force comprising two armored brigades with a total strength of 170 tanks and no more than 60 artillery pieces. These were U.S. M60 Patton and British Centurion tanks, modified and modernized. There were also various fortifications, better defended than those along the Suez Canal, but not of a significant weight. Obstacles and mines were widely seeded, and a 12-foot tank ditch spanned almost along the entire ceasefire line.

An Israeli Centurion tank

A Syrian T-62 tank

Behind the lines, at a point called Nafekh Fort, surrounded by a large military encampment, was the Golan front headquarters, and the officer commanding the northern sector was 46-year-old Major-General Yitzak Hofi. On the western slopes of Mount Hermon, at a height of about 6,500 feet, an Israeli observation point commanded a view over the entire battlefield. In its simplest terms, the Syrian strategy was to punch a hole in Israeli defenses and drive down to the east bank of the Jordan, thereby not only recapturing the Golan but placing Syrian armor and infantry in a position to menace key Israeli populations areas. The attack opened with an initial air and artillery barrage lasting about 50 minutes before the Syrians began their armored advance along a broad front. Flail-tanks and armored bulldozers preceded the advance, and within an hour, the Syrians had crossed the ceasefire line and were quickly overrunning Israeli positions. The observation post on Mount Hermon was taken after a short but ferocious commando assault, and by evening, the main Syrian effort was focused on the Tapline Road to the south and in and around the Israeli-occupied city of Quneitra to the north.

The battle ebbed and flowed, with the Syrian blunt instrument of forward-armor advance countered by desperate heroism on the part of heavily outnumbered Israeli tanks crews and displays of tank marksmanship and maneuver that certainly vindicated the tactical reputation of Israeli tank brigades. As the sun rose on the second day, it was revealed that Israeli forces had been driven back to the western edge of the Golan plateau. The Israeli 188th Armored Brigade had been effectively decimated; according to most accounts, 90 percent of the brigade's officers had been killed, and it was fielding no more than a handful of serviceable tanks. Syrian tanks were now positioned just 10 minutes advance from the east bank of the Jordan River. A Syrian effort to take the Israeli fort at Nafekh was stopped in the middle of the camp, and there, miraculously, the line held.

In the south, along the Suez front, evening brought a lull in the fighting, and as Israeli tanks withdrew, the Egyptians made good use of the hours of darkness to complete bridging operations. Thereafter, the Egyptian Second and Third Armies began to organize and consolidate in preparation for the expected Israeli counterattack.

In the meantime, assessing the losses, General Mandler reported back to Sinai command that of the 290 tanks that went into battle that afternoon, less than a third remained. The situation was critical. The mobilization of IDF reserves had begun, and armored reinforcements were beginning to arrive at the front. As Gonen and his commanders huddled around a table deep in the command bunker, trying to make sense of the battlefield, they began to formulate a response.

On the morning of October 8, having granted both themselves and the Egyptians a day to consolidate, Israeli tanks were back in action. The initial thrust of the counterattack called for the advance of a tank division, commanded by General Avraham Adan, along the main lateral road, breaking up into brigade strength to assault the enemy at three strategic points along the canal, concentrating broadly around Ismailia and the Firdan Bridge. Once again, however, the operation was launched without prior reconnaissance, and the division almost immediately found itself too far to the east, where it was moving away from the main concentrations of Egyptian force. This, when recognized and corrected, left the Israelis moving across the Egyptian front and not its flank, exposed to anti-tank artillery, after which the main attack developed east to west into positions that the Egyptians had prepared for precisely such an approach.

In a virtual replay of the day before, as an Israeli tank brigade came into range, Egyptian tank-killer teams simply stepped out of their foxholes, appearing as if out of nowhere, and unleashed a combination of missiles and rockets that quickly took 12 Israeli tanks out of commission. A division commanded by general Ariel Sharon, en route south with similar orders, was immediately diverted north to reinforce General Adan's division, which Sharon was now too far south to practically accomplish. A major battle then ensued, with Adan's division surrounded on three sides by thousands of Egyptian infantry and taking significant casualties.

Thus, the Israeli counterattack quickly began to unravel, and, of course, Sharon was enraged at the waste of his potential through contradictory orders and a fruitless series of back and forth maneuvers. Always a fiery character, Sharon was apt to express his anger without inhibition. Adan was able to withdraw, albeit with heavy losses, and at least his men had inflicted similarly heavy losses on the Egyptians. The inescapable result, however, was a failed counterattack and further unsustainable losses of Israeli men and equipment.

Sharon (right)

Israeli Prime Minister Golda Meir, a straight-talking, chain-smoking grandmother, left the military situation in the hands of her military commanders and got to work mobilizing Israeli diplomatic resources. The Israelis needed arms and resupply, and the first to be notified of this was Kissinger. Kissinger's initial perception of the battlefield was also somewhat confused and colored by the majority opinion that the Arabs would be soundly beaten sooner than later, but now he began to appreciate that this might not in fact be the case. So far, battlefield statistics were chilling. In the opening encounters on both fronts, the Israelis had lost some 50 warplanes and 500 tanks, 400 in the Sinai alone. Kissinger contacted Nixon, who happened to be embroiled in Watergate and was perhaps grateful for a distraction, and Kissinger was instructed to assure the Israelis that their needs would be met.

In Tel Aviv, meanwhile, the gravity of the situation was slowly being digested. Israel had its back against the wall, and a mood of pessimism was beginning to creep into the official exchanges. At some point, it's widely believed the question of deploying nuclear weapons as a last resort came under discussion. This has never been confirmed and in many quarters denied, especially since Israel has never publicly acknowledged having nuclear weapons, but enough anecdotal evidence and investigative reporting exists to suggest very strongly that the possibility was considered. Certainly the coded dissemination of Israel discussion about the use of nuclear weapons would have galvanized the United States to act, and that certainly seems to have happened.

While the Israelis were possibly pondering this dark scenario, Sadat was basking in the glow of military success and fielding diplomatic representation from various quarters, including Britain and the Soviet Union, probing the possibility of a ceasefire. In Sadat's mind, however, there was still more to be achieved on the battlefield. Although he had allowed himself to be cautiously optimistic, he could never have hoped for such a spectacular result. How much more could be achieved was hard to say, but for the time being, he refused to entertain any offers or overtures toward mediation. The Egyptian position was strong, and the two armies comprising the Egyptian expeditionary force were well dug in and waiting for the next phase of the war.

More interestingly, perhaps, were the coded messages beginning to arrive at Centre 10 in Cairo from Damascus. The Syrian advance on the Golan had been stopped, their positions were being held, and according to the original understanding, it was now time for Egyptian forces to begin pushing inland to seize the all-important Sinai Passes. This would require the Israelis to divert forces south to arrest the Egyptian advance, offering the opportunity for the Syrians to effect their own phase two, which was to push deeper into northern Israel with an undefined end game that could nonetheless reasonably be surmised.

Sadat, however, did not order that advance. His strategy for the moment remained at limited war in the interests of a political objective, and there would be nothing to be gained in the short term by ordering his armored divisions out from under the air shield to face Israeli armor and air power unprotected.

Meanwhile, U.S. arms supplies to Israel began reasonably quickly, with the first covert shipments handled by EL Al commercial airliners. These consisted of munitions and ordnance, rather than the tanks and aircraft so badly needed, a byproduct of the fact that concerns about the U.S./Middle East relations tended to limit immediate and direct U.S. involvement. A U.S. air bridge would simply be too high profile. However, Golda Meir was not a woman to be thwarted, and her persistent efforts and direct appeals to Nixon paid off. On October 13, a week after the first assault, the U.S. Air Force was ordered to undertake an airlift, and notwithstanding daunting logistical hurdles, Operation *Nickel Grass* swung into action. With that, the Israelis' lifeline began to flow.

An M60 being delivered as part of Operation *Nickel Grass*

A Reversal of Fortunes

"Every IDF commander was deeply imbued with the idea that we would have to cross at some point. This was an organic part of the IDF's doctrine of transferring the war to enemy territory and terminating it there quickly." - Major-General Avraham Adan

The situation in the Sinai began to stabilize on October 9, three days after the initial assault.

The arrival of Israeli reserve units steadily fortified frontline positions, and Israeli field command at last began to fully get a measure of the battlefield. Resupply was underway, and tactics were adapting.

Along the Golan, on the other hand, October 8 and 9 were pivotal days. The initial impact of the Syrian assault, stopped at the very edge of the western escarpment, was checked on October 7 by the narrowest of margins. The situation in the days that followed remained perilous, and fighting was ongoing and intense. However, Israeli reserve tank units were beginning to apply pressure, and Syrian appeals to Cairo for the long-promised commencement of the Sinai advance were going unanswered. Israeli confidence was beginning to creep back, and on the evening of October 9, an upbeat general staff meeting was held in Tel Aviv, during which the question was not whether an Israeli counter-offensive on the Golan could succeed but how far into Syria it would push.

Such too was discussion in regards to the situation in the Sinai. The Israelis were at full strength, with two additional reserve tank brigades. The lie of the battlefield was relatively simple. Two Egyptian armies were now well established on the east bank of the Suez, comprising armored, mechanized, and infantry divisions, all protected by rear artillery emplacements and anti-aircraft. That said, since the lines were static, that favored the Egyptians; the IDF was configured for mobility, and the supreme expression of that mobility would be to take the war across the Suez and into Egypt. Waiting in reserve on the Egyptian side of the canal, however, was an Egyptian reserve, the First Army, comprising the same essential compliment. A direct Israeli assault into Egypt was, therefore, not feasible until the Third Egyptian Army crossed into the Sinai. Orders, therefore, were to regroup, consolidate, and wait and allow matters on the Northern Front to resolve before dealing with the Egyptians. When the Egyptian First Army began to cross the canal, that would be the moment to hit.

The retaking of the Golan Heights and the Israeli push into Syria was a multi-faceted and complicated series of maneuvers, and in both cases the Israelis had external factors to consider when determining how far to push. An invasion of western Syria would provoke a Soviet response, which would require a U.S. response, and no one wanted that. The U.S. 6th Fleet was already circling the Soviet Mediterranean Squadron in the Mediterranean, both responding to one another's airlifts and arms resupplies, and it would take very little at that point for them to start trading punches. It was agreed in consultation with the cabinet to press the war into Syria, but not all the way to Damascus, which lay only a few dozen miles to the northeast of the Golan. That would be sufficient to panic the Syrians, cut them down to size, and perhaps goad the Egyptians into action in the Sinai.

The commencement of the Israeli counteroffensive in the Golan was planned for the morning of October 11, five days into the war. General Yitzak Hofi, commanding the northern sector, settled on a concentrated assault delivered from the north, across open country, with Mount Hermon covering the left flank of the Israeli advance. Israeli divisions would attack westward along the Israeli 91, 98, and 99 highways, the principal roads linking Israel with Syria and all leading by the shortest route to Damascus. The Syrians, having already retreated back across the ceasefire line, were dug in to prepare for the inevitable Israeli advance. The offensive was characterized by small but ferocious tank battles, often against entrenched and mechanized infantry, fought village by village and mile by mile across dense minefields and against determined Syrian opposition. These were brief but bloody engagements that exacted a heavy cost in armor and casualties on both sides. The Israelis gained territory in increments against camouflaged and emplaced Syrian armor and artillery that were by no means in disarray, but fighting an organized rear-guard action of interdiction and attrition.

The deciding battle was fought on October 13, between Israeli tanks and a detachment of Iraqi armor, drawn into a carefully concealed ambush. The Iraqis, only recently arriving on the battlefield as part of an Arab multi-national commitment, were decimated and pitched into retreat. The Israelis followed close behind and arrived that afternoon within artillery range of Damascus.

As Israeli guns opened up on the Golan, Sadat began to field more anguished appeals from Damascus to pull his armies out of their defensive positions and move against the Israelis. Sadat had refused to do this, which was wise from a military perspective. While the Egyptians were dug in, there was little that the IDF could do, but at the moment that Egyptian tanks and infantry left the cover of the missile shield, the Israelis could bring their armor and air assets to bear, and the fight would be on again.

Sadat resisted for days, but on October 12, he issued the order, and the date of the operation was set for October 14. This order was greeted with astonishment at a senior command level. A few days earlier, things might have been different, but at that moment, such an order was suicidal. Sadat, insisted, and he even threatened to issue the order himself, so in the end, the necessary orders were given. Egyptian reserve armor then began to move east across the canal, the kind of maneuver that the Israelis had been waiting for, and from then on, all IDF attention shifted to the Sinai. On October 14, Egyptian armored brigades emerged from under the cover of their anti-aircraft shields and rushed headlong into an ill-conceived series of frontal attacks, directly into pre-prepared IDF positions. Covered by withering IAF ground support, Israeli tank brigades went into action, and within a few hours, Egyptian armored capability was practically destroyed. By the evening of October 14, Egyptian forces were ordered back to the cover of their bridgeheads, deeply shocked. A brief hiatus followed as the Israelis waited for the expected follow-up, but the Egyptians were beaten.

The Israeli high command was quick to grasp the fact that the tide of war had shifted. Approval was sought to cross into Egypt, which was granted on October 15. The plan was for an Israeli armored division to cross the Suez at the junction between the Egyptian Second (north) and Third (south) armies, with a view to encircling the western flank of the Third Army by the capture of the Egyptian city of Suez. The crossing was to take place at a section of the canal slightly above the north shore of the Bitter Lakes, known as Chinese Farm, which would cover the left flank, leaving the right flank, which was also the southern rump of the Second Army, to be defended by a tank detachment. Once across, Israeli forces would circle south behind enemy lines and effectively cut off the Third Army from retreat, isolate it from resupply, and in effect, hold it hostage. This would grant Israel a very strong hand in any future negotiation and would most certainly bring about an end to the war.

A picture of Israeli tanks crossing the Suez Canal

It is possible that the crossing was premature, and there certainly was a risk of isolating Israeli units in Egyptian territory if the rearguard failed to hold. This rearguard has since entered Israeli military lore as one of the greatest and most costly battles of this and other wars. A large tank detachment was positioned to contain the southern positions of the Egyptian Second Army, an action that devolved into a bitter and brutal tank duel lasting most of the night. Of the aftermath of this battle, the Battle of Chinese Farm, General Ariel Sharon would later recall in his memoir *Warrior*: "The morning of October 16 dawned on the most terrible sight I have ever seen. All that night Ammon's brigade, along with several paratrooper elements, the remnants of Yoav Broms reconnaissance unit, one of Tuvia's battalions and one of Haim Erez's, had been engaged with the better part of two Egyptian divisions."

The net result, however, was that Israeli tank units successfully crossed the Suez into Egypt and, circling to the south, advanced on the city of Suez. This was a bold and innovative military maneuver, an expression of Israeli mobile armored tactics at their best. The effect of it was to swing Israeli forces behind the Egyptian Third Army, deployed along the southern sector of the canal on the north shore of the Gulf of Suez. The entire Third Army was now effectively cut off from retreat, and although ground commanders sought permission to press the advantage further, what had been achieved in this single maneuver provided ample leverage for a political solution to end the fighting.

The Aftermath

"We can forgive the Arabs for killing our children. We cannot forgive them for forcing us to kill their children." – Golda Meir

By the time the Israelis had successfully fought their way across the Suez, the situation in Syria had stabilized, and Israeli forces on the outskirts of Damascus dug in and made the most of a commanding position. Like Assad, Sadat was shocked at the news of the sudden and dramatic defeat of his armies in the Sinai, and his response was immediately to petition the Soviet Union to convene an emergency meeting of the UN Security Council to secure an immediate ceasefire.

In conjunction with that, Arab oil-producing states raised the price of oil by 70 percent, threatening at the same time a 5 percent cut in production for every month that Israel remained in the territories occupied during the Six-Day War. The next day, on October 18, the Saudi government went further, announcing a 10 percent cut in oil output. A day later, President Richard Nixon formally requested Congress to authorize a $2.2 billion emergency aid package for Israel, and Saudi Arabia responded by placing an oil embargo on the United States. Other Arab countries soon followed. The market ramifications were heavy, and Nixon was obliged, in the midst of the Watergate scandal, to divert his full attention to the crisis in the Middle East.

By now, just about everyone wanted to bring the whole episode to a close. On October 19, Kissinger flew to Moscow for talks, and the next day, Sadat was informed that both superpowers were committed to the implementation of a ceasefire. Kissinger then traveled to Israel to present the plan to the Israeli cabinet, while Soviet officials headed to Cairo to deliver Sadat more or less the same message. These visits were, superficially at least, described as consultative, but neither side in the war could, nor perhaps would, have contested a ceasefire. And while threats and counter-threats continued to reverberate across the battlefield, for the most part both sides froze their positions in place and waited.

On October 22, 1973, the Israeli cabinet formally accepted the ceasefire, but, enraged at being held back within striking distance of Suez, the Israeli advance column felt pressure to keep the fight moving. On October 22, Israeli Prime Minister Golda Meir, anxious to complete the encirclement of the Egyptian Third Army before operations ceased, tacitly granted permission for the advance to continue, stirring such shrill appeals from Cairo that, after a brief exchange of accusations and counter-accusations, a second ceasefire came into effect on October 25. This was followed soon afterward by the deployment of a United Nations monitoring force, and under international pressure, the Israelis partially lifted the siege of Suez City, allowing UN relief supplies to reach the civilian population. In the end, a series of disengagement of forces agreements between Egypt, Syria, and Israel were signed on January 18 and May 31 in 1974. Only then did the IDF stand down and release its reserves.

In the long post-mortem that followed, the Israelis accepted international congratulations for a great military achievement, and the reputation of the IDF suffered very little as a consequence of the narrow margin by which the war had been won. Over 2,800 Israelis lost their lives, with three times that number wounded and perhaps 500 taken as prisoners of war.[16] Given Israel's small population, this loss was keenly felt, and the Israeli post-mortem of the period involved a great deal of self-searching. A commission of inquiry was held, the Agranat Commission, to determine where failures had occurred, and while almost the entire senior command suffered some degree of censure, the most severe criticism was reserved for the Director General for Military Intelligence, General Eli Zeira, whose career never recovered. Perhaps the most important impact of the war on the Israeli psyche, however, was to wipe away the myth of the IDF's invincibility and shock the nation out of some of its complacency. Moreover, as Sadat anticipated, it would prompt the Israeli political and general establishment to view negotiations with the Arabs in a more favorable light.

In 1976, Jimmy Carter was elected president, and Sadat was determined to build a positive and personal relationship with the new leader of the United States. By this time, the Soviet Union had all but cut off its relations with Egypt; for years, the Soviet bloc had assumed that Egypt was in its sphere of influence, but the expulsion of Soviet advisors from Egypt, Sadat's complete disregard for Soviet warnings not to engage Israel in war, and Sadat's newfound friendship with

---

[16] Casualty listings for Egypt note 5,000 deaths and Syria, 8,000. Iraq reported an improbable 5,000 deaths and Jordan, 1,000.

Kissinger and his active involvement in the U.S.-led Egyptian-Israeli peace efforts were the final straws. To the chagrin of many Arab states, Sadat realized that the U.S. was the only country in the world with the resources, power, and influence to guide Israel and Egypt toward full peace. As Sadat later wrote, "He who cannot change the very fabric of his thought will never be able to change reality, and will never, therefore, make any progress."[17]

Sadat and Carter

Among all the dramatic actions Sadat took during his presidency – from his fiery decision to oust all Soviet advisors from Egypt to his audacious gamble with the Yom Kippur War -- certainly the most dramatic and breathtaking one was his decision to visit Jerusalem. It must be noted that none of Sadat's decisions, including this one, were ever executed on whim or without much thought; Sadat's symbolic visit to Israel – the first visit an Arab leader made to Israeli soil – was calculated and well thought-out. In one simple gesture, Sadat irrevocably changed the nature and tone of the long-running Arab-Israeli conflict, granting Israel the recognition they had been demanding for decades while proving to his newfound ally, the United States, and to the world that Egypt was committed to peace. Against the advice of his aides and the wishes of his fellow Arab heads of state, on November 19, 1977, Sadat landed in Jerusalem.[18]

When Sadat returned to Cairo, he was welcomed by an electrified population and a parliament that was nearly in full agreement to endorse his actions. Beyond question or doubt, Sadat's visit to Jerusalem was one of the greatest milestones of the twentieth century, becoming a cornerstone in the modern history of the Middle East. But in the months that followed, negotiations with Israel, again facilitated by the U.S., stalled again over the Palestinian issue and territorial disputes. In September 1978, with the hope to finally settle a peace treaty once and for all, President Jimmy Carter invited Sadat and Israeli Prime Minister Begin to Camp David in Washington D.C. For 11 days, the three leaders negotiated, discussed, and argued.

On September 17, 1978, the two sides were finally able to agree on a framework for peace. In short, the framework stipulated that Israel will execute a full withdrawal from the Sinai

---

[17] Carroll, *Anwar Sadat*, 81.
[18] Elbendary, "The Long Revolution."

Peninsula over a three-year period, while Egypt would develop full peaceful relations with Israel. The fact that there should be transitional agreements established for the West Bank and Gaza, and for continued discussion over the status of Palestinians and Jewish settlers in the occupied territories, was also included.[19] As vague as this framework was, it was an essential step in the peace process, and it ultimately led to the March 1979 signing of the Egyptian-Israeli Peace Treaty.

Sadat, Carter, and Begin shake hands at the ceremony announcing the peace agreement

The normalization of relations between Israel and Egypt went into effect in January 1980, but during the final months of Sadat's life, internal opposition was beginning to form. Sadat brushed this aside as just another Soviet plot to destabilize this government, but rumors of a plot organized by Egyptian dissidents living abroad to overthrow Sadat emerged. Undeterred, Sadat continued to focus on foreign affairs and the peace effort.[20]

On October 6, 1981, Anwar Sadat was assassinated during a victory parade honoring the eighth anniversary of the Yom Kippur War. In shocking footage that spread across the world, Sadat and spectators near him were attacked by some of the parade's participants, and as they approached Sadat's position firing weapons, Sadat actually thought it was part of the parade and stood up to salute them. In addition to firing with automatic weapons, grenades were thrown into the crowd as well. Egyptian security forces eventually engaged the assassins and killed and wounded some of them, but Sadat had been mortally wounded in the attack. Hosni Mubarak, who would succeed Sadat and go on to rule Egypt for decades, was also injured in the attack.

Although he will always be remembered for his courage and boldness, for his significant role in global diplomacy, and his hard-earned achievements in the peace process, Anwar Sadat's

---

[19] "The Camp David Accords of 1979," *BBC News*, November 29, 2001,
http://news.bbc.co.uk/2/hi/in_depth/middle_east/israel_and_the_palestinians/key_documents/1632849.stm.
[20] Pace, "Anwar El-Sadat, the Daring Arab Pioneer of Peace with Israel."

ultimate legacy remains uncertain, even today. The negotiations that were begun by Sadat have achieved neither a resolution nor an amelioration of the Arab-Israeli conflict. He left behind a tense and difficult relationship, in which he himself was a key part that held it together. So strongly had Sadat fought for peace that he began to personify it; upon Sadat's death, the Israelis' confidence in continued efforts for peace with his successor Hosni Mubarak dwindled. Campaigns emerged in Israel to block the withdrawal process from the Sinai – a key component of the 1979 peace treaty. As Israeli Interior Minister Yosef Burg put it aptly, "We shall find out if a man or an idea was killed."[21]

Sadat also left behind an isolated Egypt – an outcast among its fellow Arab states. The treaty with Israel had been costly; Egypt was suspended from the Arab League in 1979, and political alliances realigned and shifted against Egyptian interests.[22] It would be years before the Arab League would lift the suspension and Egypt returned to its position as a dominant player in the region.

Despite the concerns in the wake of Sadat's assassination, one of his primary goals for the Yom Kippur War was eventually realized. The Sinai was demilitarized, and on April 25, 1982, Israel withdrew the last of its troops from the peninsula.

Online Resources

Other Middle Eastern history titles by Charles River Editors

Other titles about the Six Day War on Amazon

Other titles about the Yom Kippur War on Amazon

Further Reading

Barzilai, Gad (1996). Wars, Internal Conflicts, and Political Order: A Jewish Democracy in the Middle East. New York University Press. ISBN 978-0-7914-2944-0

Cristol, A Jay (2002). Liberty Incident: The 1967 Israeli Attack on the U.S. Navy Spy Ship. Brassey's. ISBN 1-57488-536-7

Finkelstein, Norman (June 2017). Analysis of the war and its aftermath, on the 50th anniversary of the June 1967 war (3 parts, each about 30 min)

Gat, Moshe (2003). Britain and the Conflict in the Middle East, 1964–1967: The Coming of the Six-Day War. Praeger/Greenwood. ISBN 0-275-97514-2

Hammel, Eric (October 2002). "Sinai air strike: June 5, 1967". Military Heritage. 4 (2): 68–73.

Herzog, Chaim (1982). The Arab-Israeli Wars. Random House. ISBN 978-0-394-50379-0.

Herzog, Chaim (1989). Heroes of Israel. Boston: Little, Brown. ISBN 0-316-35901-7.

Hopwood, Derek (1991). Egypt: Politics and Society. London: Routledge. ISBN 0-415-09432-1

Hussein of Jordan (1969). My "War" with Israel. London: Peter Owen. ISBN 0-7206-0310-2

Israelyan, Victor (2003) [1995]. Inside the Kremlin During the Yom Kippur War. University Park, PA: Pennsylvania State University Press. ISBN 0-271-01737-6.

Katz, Samuel M. (1991) Israel's Air Force; The Power Series. Motorbooks International Publishers & Wholesalers, Osceola, WI.

Makiya, Kanan (1998). Republic of Fear: The Politics of Modern Iraq. University of California Press. ISBN 0-520-21439-0

---

[21] Carroll, *Anwar Sadat*, 104.

[22] John Kifner, "Confrontation in the Gulf; Badly Divided Arab League Votes to Return Headquarters to Cairo," *The New York Times*, September 11, 1990, http://www.nytimes.com/1990/09/11/world/confrontation-gulf-badly-divided-arab-league-votes-return-headquarters-cairo.html.

Morris, Benny (1997). Israel's Border Wars, 1949–1956. Oxford: Oxford University Press. ISBN 0-19-829262-7

Pressfield, Steven (2014). The Lion's Gate: On the Front Lines of the Six Day War. Sentinel HC, 2014. ISBN 1-59523-091-2

Rabinovich, Abraham (2005) [2004]. The Yom Kippur War: The Epic Encounter That Transformed the Middle East. New York, NY: Schocken Books. ISBN 0-8052-4176-0.

Rezun, Miron (1990). "Iran and Afghanistan." In A. Kapur (Ed.). Diplomatic Ideas and Practices of Asian States (pp. 9–25). Brill Academic Publishers. ISBN 90-04-09289-7

Shazly, Lieutenant General Saad el (2003). The Crossing of the Suez, Revised Edition (Revised ed.). American Mideast Research. ISBN 0-9604562-2-8.

Shlaim, Avi (2001). The Iron Wall: Israel and the Arab World. W. W. Norton & Company. ISBN 0-393-32112-6.

Smith, Grant (2006). Deadly Dogma. Institute for Research: Middle Eastern Policy. ISBN 0-9764437-4-0

Oren, Michael (April 2002). Six Days of War: June 1967 and the Making of the Modern Middle East. Oxford University Press.

Free Books by Charles River Editors

We have brand new titles available for free most days of the week. To see which of our titles are currently free, click on this link.

Discounted Books by Charles River Editors

We have titles at a discount price of just 99 cents everyday. To see which of our titles are currently 99 cents, click on this link.